CURING URBANITIS
THE METROPOLITAN DISEASE
Tough Love Remedies for Big City Problems

William E. Finley

ISBN: 1-4196-9218-6
ISBN-13: 9781419692185

Visit www.booksurge.com to order additional copies.

Urbanitis is defined as a disease or condition affecting American metropolitan areas experiencing the uncontrolled spreading of urban growth, stressful traffic congestion, dangerous inner-city neighborhoods, worsening air pollution, and inadequate tax resources.

Although the majority of the U.S. population lives in metropolitan areas, at the present time, there is no holistic plan or approach to combat these conditions.

Cover photos: Airphotos-Jim Wark and Cathi Milenas

Background Statement of William E. Finley

Born Chicago, IL, October 29, 1923. Grad.Washington HS, Milwaukee, WI, June 1942. Enlisted as Air Cadet, US Army Air Corps, Inducted Jan 1943. Completed pilot training, Feb 1944. Joined 8th Air Force in England, July 1944; completed thirty-five missions including shuttle mission to Warsaw/USSR/Italy. Awarded five Air Medals, three Battle stars, and two Unit Commendations. Honorably Discharged May, 1946.

Education: Received A.B. (1949) and Masters degree in City and Regional Planning (1951) at the University of California at Berkeley. Completed graduate work for advanced degree in Gerontology at Lynn University, Boca Raton, FL (1990).

Leadership Positions in City and Regional Planning:
1951 Asst. & Planning Director, City of Richmond, CA; Emphasis on urban redevelopment.

1956 Project Director, New Town in Ravenswood, WV, for Kaiser Aluminum: Planned town, acquired site, initiated residential development.

1958 Director, National Capital Planning Commission, Wash. DC; Emphasis on mass transportation plan, urban redevelopment & reg. planning; Principal Author: *The Year 2000 Plan for the Nation's Capital.* 1959 Vice Chair, National Capital Housing Authority, Washington, DC.

1960 Interim Consultant, Community Redevelopment Advisor to Governor of American Samoa. Prepared Rebuilding Plan for capital, Pago Pago, for Pacific Area Conference.

Leadership Positions in Management of Community Development:
1962 Vice President, The Rouse Company; Project Director, Village of Cross Keys, Baltimore, MD. 1963 Senior Project Director, new town of Columbia, 14,000 acres, Howard County, MD. Emphasis on innovative social, economic and physical planning, preservation of open space, open housing, job generation, cultural facilities and advanced management systems for complex development project.

1972 President/General Mgr. InterAmerican Trade and Cultural Authority (INTERAMA) State of Florida, Independent Development Authority in North Miami, FL. Emphasis on planning, design and construction of the

$200 million trade, education and entertainment complex on 550 acres in Biscayne Bay. Project cancelled when State failed to provide funding.

1974 President, Cedar-Riverside Redevelopment Partnership, Minneapolis, MN. Emphasis on rescuing $100+ million urban redevelopment project from mismanagement, environmental lawsuits and governmental interference. Achieved interim refinancing to extend life of project.

1976 Executive Vice President, Horizon Corporation, developer of 25,000 acre recreation community north of Houston, TX. Emphasis on designing and building new housing products, aggressive new concepts in marketing and reorganization of the development team.

1980 President, Bankers Land Company, Florida real estate subsidiary of Chicago-based John D. & Catherine T. MacArthur Foundation that owned 46,000 acres in Palm Beach and Martin Counties; FL.. Emphasis on new community planning, disposition of properties, setting standards for regional commercial complex and representing the Foundation in South Florida.

1988 Executive Director, Community Redevelopment Agency and Downtown Development Authority, Delray Beach, FL. Emphasis on redevelopment plan for problem area affecting larger community, marketing the Downtown shopping street and encouraging celebrations to enhance the community.

1990 Project Manager, Inskoy New Town, Kemerova region, Siberia, Russian Federation. Emphasis on new town plan, land assembly, housing design for subzero winters, shipping and assembling panelized single family dwellings for coal mining families.

1992 Executive Director, Homestead Economic Recovery Organization (HERO), Homestead, FL, town of 25,000 flattened by Hurricane Andrew. Project managed under the aegis of the Enterprise Foundation. Emphasis on preparation of redeveloprnent plan, allocation of resources to categories of rebuilding projects including single family, apartments, commercial and industrial buildings and devastated Downtown area.

1996 Owner-Developer, Oceanfront townhouse development, Gulf-stream, FL.

2000 Executive Vice President, The Arena on Clematis; Based on winning a competition for developers to finance, construct and manage a 10,000 seat multi-purpose arena to serve Palm Beach County, public-private financing for the arena was arranged, construction plans were initiated and a development schedule was set. The project was cancelled when a third party volunteered to build an arena without cost to the County.

2001 Consulting Project Manager, under contract to FEMA to rebuild Princeville, NC, an historic African-American town flooded out by hurricane-related coastal storms in Eastern North Carolina. Project team completed relocation surveys of dislocated people, inventories of buildings and plans for rebuilding. FEMA made grants to the local community and contracts were executed with reconstruction companies.

Teaching Positions

1949 Teaching Assistant, new Department of City and Regional Planning, University of California at Berkeley, CA.

1953 Lecturer, Lifelong Learning Extension, University of California, Oakland, CA.

1957 Visiting Professor, Department of City Planning, College of Fine Arts, University of Pennsylvania, Philadelphia, PA.

1989 Lecturer, Graduate course on Housing the Elderly, Lynn University, Boca Raton FL.

2001 Seminar Instructor, International City Managers' Association, USAID-sponsored seminars in seven cities in Bulgaria, including Sofia, for former Communist officials assigned to manage the redevelopment of their cities. Emphasis on urban history of America, legal bases for redevelopment and methodologies for public-private partnerships.

Activities in Publishing

1990 Co-Founder and Co-Publisher, developed a magazine dedicated to serving originally the senior population and eventually the Baby Boomer generation. Magazine in its eighteenth year of publication.

1992 Co-Author, *Live To Be 100 PLUS*, a how-to book on the steps to greater longevity.

1996 Co-Publisher, *Creating the New City*, Edited by Robert Tennenbaum

1999 Columnist, *"Living the New Millennium" in Boomer Times & Senior Life*, a South Florida magazine.

Leadership in Community Affairs

1987 Board Chairman (11 yrs), The Armory Arts Center, a community arts-making and exhibition center.

1982 Founder/First President, SunFest, the largest Spring, musical, ethnic foods and juried art show in Florida celebrating its twenty-fifth anniversary, drew 350,000 visitors in 2007.

1982 Founding Board Member, Neighbors Organized for Adequate Housing (NOAH), a non-profit housing group in Belle Glade, FL.

1986 Founder/First Executive Director/current Chairman, The Housing Partnership, Inc. a non-profit organization dedicated to financing and building affordable housing and assisting families to prepare themselves for home ownership.

Table of Contents

Chapter 1. Inaugural speech of the 44th President, January 20, 2009   19
"I, too, have a dream ..." The President proposes new policies to control urban growth in metropolitan areas.

Chapter 2. The Torrential Expansion of Suburbia   25
It spells out all the elements fueling suburban expansion and describes the power of the forces that keep it going without regard for crumbling center cities, the endless destruction of urban sprawl, and the need for workable alternatives.

Chapter 3. Curing Urbanitis in the Inner City   39
It is mainly poor Black Americans who are left behind as suburbia grows with the center city government inheriting the problems. Both the center city and the outlying governments resist serious regional planning and action for very different reasons.

Chapter 4. The Waves on the Horizon   53
The absolute certainty that the next 100 million people will head for the already strained metropolitan areas should warn their government and business leaders that trouble is on the way.

Chapter 5. Curing Urbanitis at the Regional Scale   63
Metropolitan-wide analysis, planning, and restructuring will be essential if any progress is to be made in solving the major growth problems. Criteria are spelled out on how to go about such a process and what the positive and negative outcomes might be.

Chapter 6. Launching the New MetroCities   75
This is the "how to" methodology describing what it will take to locate, plan, and initiate community development of new metropolitan areas of 500,000 each. An illustrative budget is included as well as a realistic timetable.

Chapter 7. A Public-Private Partnership to Lead the Way   93
Based on the success and failures of various entities to undertake enormous tasks, a form of non-profit previously used by the Government

is proposed. A unique joint funding plan is structured to utilize the strength of each party and avoid their pitfalls.

Chapter 8. Lessons Learned from New Towns   103
Based on fifty years' experience in planning and building English and American New Towns, an arsenal of management and technology is available to create the teams needed to initiate the new MetroCities. A special section on the unique Columbia Planning Process is related.

Chapter 9. The Science of Locating New MetroCities   125
This broad set of activities would result in extensive research on where such major new metropolitan cities could be built for the benefit of the existing regions wishing to redirect some growth and the positive impacts on the communities in and around the chosen locations.

Chapter 10. A Fork in the Road   133
Recommended National Policies on Urban Growth. The focus here is on choices metropolitan areas are faced with, to continue with sprawl and its serious consequences or to step up to new ways to develop and the extraordinary benefits in taking the right road. To assist leaders to be clear about the issues, a draft of proposed Federal policies is offered.

Chapter 11. A Timetable for Action   141
An optimistic timetable is laid out for the next twenty years calling for Presidential leadership and Congressional action. Potential positive outcomes are described but likely pitfalls are pointed out.

Chapter 12. *The year 2000 Plan for the Nation's Capital*   147
Excerpts from the Plan document spell out the power and value of bold regional planning and the positive impact it can have on the growth of the metropolitan area. In the Washington region, the multi-billion dollar mass transit system was planned and built to conform to the adopted regional plan.

Chapter 13. The New South Richmond Project   167
The Mayor of New York City requested that The Rouse Company utilize its planning and development skills to find a way to redevelop the largely vacant southern one-third of Staten Island. Although the project was never built, the report spelling out the alternatives and

the fiscal impact of each is a world-class analysis and financial model for any large urban project including new metropolitan areas.

Postscript   181

Bibliography   183

Index   191

Introduction

Although the United States is not noted for planning ahead, it is famous for its capacity to react powerfully to an urgent challenge. Faced with official predictions of another 100 million population over the next few decades, most metropolitan areas are already experiencing uncontrolled and costly suburban development and increasing poverty and crime levels in their center cities. Yet, it would seem that most lack the vision to correct these threatening trends.

The reasons for the absence of serious metropolitan-wide concerns include acceptance of the run-down conditions of the center city, the insular attitudes of the suburban governments and the complete lack of urban leadership at the State and Federal levels. Regional thinking is largely limited to matters of transportation, water and sewer systems, and half-hearted efforts to combat air pollution.

A powerful force for continuing suburban expansion consists of the parties that benefit the most: large landowners, housing and commercial builders, design and construction companies, and the financial institutions that provide short-term financing and long-term mortgages. Unfortunately, there are no equal forces eager and able to demand a true list of mounting costs of current trends and capable of suggesting alternatives to urban sprawl and acceptable living conditions of urban minorities.

Economists and social scientists have testified to the growing human, social, and financial costs of the trends that produce more and more homes, stores, industrial space, and commercial outlets spreading across the countryside. Only architects and planners have prescribed more community-minded solutions, but they only deal with the bits and pieces of urbanization. Missing or silent are the big-picture thinkers, the educators, or the writers who have seen the destructive mega-cities of Latin America or the Far East.

It may take conservative minds to question the wisdom of endless suspicions that current trends are more than wasteful, possibly unsustainable and bound to raise taxes. Amazingly enough, there is no national, public, or private entity that researches and produces findings about the coming plight of metropolitan areas. HUD is supposed to do it, but it is a weak agency that concentrates on affordable housing and guaranteeing home loans wherever a builder or lender requests.

This book will shine spotlights on these interlocked problems and offer a technically and financially feasible set of alternative futures. However, as we know, political will only comes into being either when a crisis occurs or when enough voices are raised to get the attention of business and political leaders. If a combination of Governors, U.S. Senators and Representatives, and Business leaders (not benefiting from sprawl) could focus on these urban growth issues the way they have jumped on climate change and going green, conferences would be held, regional entities would be energized, and the media would get the message.

A third major section of this book proposes the building of new "MetroCities" in undeveloped areas where they could both succeed as new community enterprises and absorb some portion of the coming population waves that would otherwise add to the woes of existing metropolitan areas. The proposed organizational, developmental and financial aspects of such a huge task are spelled out in detail based on the experiences with new towns in both the U.S. and Great Britain. Illustrative locations for the first eight new "MetroCities" are indicated on a map of the U.S. on the cover

The last two chapters cover models for regional thinking, one describing a long-range plan for the Washington, DC, region, approved by President Kennedy in 1961, that became the framework for the construction of the metropolitan transit system. The second is the conceptual plan for a city of 250,000 people proposed in 1970, for the southern third of New York City's Staten Island. It is a sophisticated financial model illustrative of the planning that would be required for new "MetroCities."

The term "Tough Love" certainly applies to the demanding nature of the solutions to big city problems, as proposed here. Local governments and State legislatures, especially, are just going about their narrow businesses and are failing to study and raise questions about the larger issues of the metropolitan trends. We hope this book will stir the pot.

William E. Finley
Ocean Ridge, FL

Acknowledgements

<u>Early mentors</u>
My mother, Myrtle Catherine Keating Finley Shankus, who waited on tables from 1932 to 1939 as a single Mom to support her only child; Uncle Jack Hosmer, my first male role model, who taught me to pilot an airplane when I was sixteen; my second role model, the manager of the National Tea Company grocery store where I worked during high school.

<u>Adult Mentors</u>
L. Deming Tilton, first Planning Director for San Francisco, who taught the first class in City Planning, 1947-49, at the University of California at Berkeley; Professor Jack Kent, second San Francisco Planning Director and Chair of the new Department of City and Regional Planning at Berkeley; Catherine Bauer Wurster, national housing expert who chaired my thesis committee at Berkeley; Wayne E. Thompson, City manager of Richmond and Oakland, CA; Richard Graves, former head of the League of California Cities and Gubernatorial candidate in 1956; Harold F. Wise, Planning Consultant, who sent me to plan and start construction of a new town for Kaiser Aluminum in Ravenswood, WV; Professors Robert Mitchell and William Wheaton, who invited me to serve as a Visiting Professor in the College of Fine Arts at the University of Pennsylvania in Philadelphia; Harland Bartholomew, appointed by Presidents Truman and Eisenhower to serve as Chair of the National Capital Planning Commission in Washington, DC, who invited me to serve as Director of that agency from 1958 to the end of 1962.

In planning this book, I called on several former colleagues and friends on concepts, content, and emphases. They were Bob Tennenbaum, Ed West, Bill Jacobson, Allan Borut, Dan O'Connell, Richard Browne, John Corbett, Pat McNamara, and Carl House. All were generous with their time and criticism. Daily advice came from Anita Finley, a publisher, writer, and observer of our urban world.

Dedication

This book and the presentation of its concepts are dedicated to:

James W. Rouse, BS, University of Maryland School of Law, 1937, who was an urban visionary who saw no reason why American cities should be places of poverty, fear, or squalid slums. He led the way through his business successes in mortgage banking, regional shopping centers, festival market places and, especially, to the conception, financing, and development of the new city of Columbia, MD, acclaimed as the most holistically planned community of 100,000 in the United States. After retiring from The Rouse Company, he launched a nation-wide campaign, through the Enterprise Foundation, to improve housing for the poor. His thoughtful, humanistic, and gentle leadership has inspired the author for over fifty years.

Anita R. Finley, MPS, Gerontologist/Publisher, my wife of thirty-three years, who has provided me with undaunted support and encouragement in many endeavors including her wise judgment regarding key aspects of this book.

And, to many friends, especially those who doubt whether these concepts regarding urban reform will ever come about, and with apologies to Eleanor Roosevelt,

IT IS BETTER TO LIGHT A ROMAN
CANDLE THAN TO CURSE THE DARKNESS

William E. Finley
June 2008

Chapter 1.
I, too, have a dream...

Scene: Washington, DC, Tuesday, January 20, 2009, on the steps of the Capitol, at the inauguration ceremony for the 44th President of the United States. After the swearing in, the new President addresses the Nation. After declaring the intentions of the incoming Administration on the global issues like the wars, climate change, health care, immigration and the economy, the President says:

"With a bow to the 1963 unforgettable declarations by Martin Luther King, Jr., who said, 'I have a dream,' as he spoke most eloquently of the need for true equality for his people. He further said, 'It is a dream deeply rooted in the American dream.'

"I, too have a dream. It has to do with the quality of life for tens of millions of Americans who live and work in our largest metropolitan areas. Many of these regions have or will soon be reaching breaking points in grid-locked traffic, unhealthy air, permanently overcrowded schools and neighborhoods, where housing conditions, chronic unemployment, and the concentration of crime create a dangerous and fearful environment.

"As our Nation's population grows from 300 million to 400 million over the next twenty-five to thirty years, these metropolitan areas will be magnets for our grandchildren and their children as well as for the legions of immigrants attracted to our shores from dozens of countries.

"Metropolitan communities take great pride in announcing the newest census figures, as if greater numbers of homes, apartments, shopping centers and big boxes actually added to the quality of life in that area. In fact, uncontrolled growth, although welcomed by those involved, will most likely make the area worse off.

"Except in the fields of transportation, environmental pollution, and utility services, where Federal mandates apply, there are no incentives for the surrounding communities to participate in solving social or economic problems of the center city. We hear little about the possibilities of limiting urban growth.

"My dream for American cities calls for looking ahead and asking leaders in every metropolitan area to reach across boundaries, to share goals and problems and to forge new mechanisms to deal with both troubled neighborhoods and methods to ensure that the coming waves of people do not engulf the social, educational, and technical systems that may already be strained. We will propose Federal incentives for the regions that make progress on these issues, possibly at the expense of those who ignore the challenge.

"I believe that the job of the President is to not only deal with current urgent problems but to look ahead and steer resources to head off difficulties clearly apparent on the horizon. Therefore, my dream envisions a bold new plan to create new metropolitan areas to help absorb a portion of the coming urban growth.

"These new pollution-free metropolitan cities could have future populations of 500,000 each and would be located beyond commuting distances of those existing, already-crowded urban areas. We will be offering details on a new public-private organization to undertake both the task of assisting metropolitan areas to deal with inner city problems and methods for controlling growth and the planning and management required to build the new communities.

"To carry out this ambitious plan, in a few months, we will be sending Congress our recommendations on how to deal with these problems that are affecting our growing cities.

"My dream is that in one generation, we will reform our worse neighborhoods, uplift its citizens, discover ways to control urban growth, and create beautiful, clean cities that will make our Country proud.

"Let us work together to make these dreams come true."

Observation
"America is a Metropolitan Nation"

The renowned and highly respected non-profit Brookings Institution in Washington, DC, has launched a major research and educational campaign under the title of a Metropolitan Policy Program that examines the resources, economies, and trends of social changes of America's 100 largest metropolitan areas.

Its findings and recommendations closely parallel the independent research and conclusions reached in this work, Curing Urbanitis, especially the emphasis on the urgent need for the Federal government to exercise its potential leadership and financial participation in turning around the direction most metropolitan areas are taking.

Brookings places heavy emphasis on the powerful roles America's metropolitan areas play in driving the national economy, particularly its capacity to regain leadership and competitive position in the global economy. Its comprehensive approach is titled, "Blueprint for American Prosperity," and strongly suggests that the Nation's financial future is closely tied to the ability of the metropolitan areas to grasp the opportunities for change and reformation.

Brookings' population projections closely correlate with the Census Bureau's indication of a U.S. population of 420 million by 2050. Their message pinpoints the critical need for increasing the quality of American human resources through a variety of educational and training programs to uplift the value of the labor force.

Expanding on the enormous importance of American metropolitan areas, its studies focus on the power of the labor markets, the housing markets and the cultural values inherent in individuals' identity with their regions. It also states that many economic regions are affected by purely localized land use decisions resulting in a serious lack of affordable housing for the very population essential for healthy economic growth.

Their studies reveal that "despite their collective potency, U.S. metros as a group are underperforming in some key measures of productive, inclusive, and sustainable growth." Their failings include an inability to maintain employment, standards of living or levels of educational attainment. The famed "middle class" continues its decline, credit ratings are slipping, and transportation delays and costs are soaring.

Among its most important but not surprising recommendations are directed at the absence of Federal awareness or leadership in moving the metro areas upward from their clear declines. Their report concludes that Brookings' Blueprint for American Prosperity "will identify reforms needed to unleash productive, inclusive, and sustainable growth well into the 21st Century."

The nation is fortunate to have such a distinguished research and educational institution focusing on the problems and opportunities presented by our metropolitan areas.

Observation
The Practical Side of the American Dream

The human side of these massive trends can be found in the Rivera Family. In 1964, Daniel met Angela at church. After graduating from high school, she became a teller at a local bank and lived with her parents in the neighborhood where she grew up. Daniel went to the Junior College for two years studying computer maintenance. He easily found a job in the downtown of their city. She walked to work and he used his ten-year old car for work.

They married and found a small apartment near both their jobs. By scrimping, their savings grew. Many of their friends talked about buying homes in the suburbs, so they got the bug and found a house they could barely afford over twenty miles from their jobs. Daniel needed a new car and found easy financing. He dropped Angela at the bank every morning and went off to his computer company. He was then promoted, but his new job required him to be away overnight at least once a week. Covering his region required their only car.

Angela tried using the bus to get to work when Daniel was away, but the service was minimal and often made her late. She applied for a transfer to a branch bank much closer to their home. It was granted the same day she found out she was pregnant. The bank's policy required her to take a leave of absence after her seventh month.

Daniel was promoted again with a slight raise in pay but was on the road three nights a week. Angela needed a car to get to see her parents and sisters and to visit the doctor. Even a car with 50,000 miles on it strained their budget. Their property taxes were raised to pay for new schools in their subdivision. In a few years, they would need that school.

Soon, the combination of mortgage payments, utility bills, car repairs, and doctors' bills forced them to turn to credit cards to save their marriage and their lives.

Chapter 2.
The Torrential Expansion of Suburbia

Spirited by the flush of military victory in World War II and in the absence of a predicted post-war depression, veterans of both the military and wartime industrial expansion spawned an optimistic economy never before experienced in America.

As women returned to home management and ready to make up for lost time in having babies, they and their eager husbands rocketed up the birthrate that became the Baby Boom generation. As the American Dream flourished, government-insured mortgages made it possible for a young couple to purchase a home they could afford.

Prior to the war, most houses were built by carpenters who would pull in plumbers and electricians to finish the job. Typically, a master carpenter would build three to five homes a year. But the war effort had required contractors to build thousands of barracks and apartment complexes for shipyard and other workers. That capacity launched a new industry, just in time to house the Boomer generation.

For the first time in history, a new industry sprang up with the capacity to finance the purchase of large tracts, use elementary prefabrication methods, and quickly produce thousands of homes fully equipped with picket fences and time-saving appliances. At the same time, installment type financing allowed young people to buy a car on time.

The concept of an Interstate Highway system actually originated with the nation's truckers' association in carrying out their plans to supplant the railroads as the carriers of bulky materials. However, the roads of America were in terrible and muddy condition. Actually, the super-highway idea was presented to President Roosevelt in 1940 who pointed out that all the steel and concrete in America would be needed in the coming war with Germany and Japan.

The super-highway plan (modeled after the German autobahn) envisioned that a trucker could drive from New York to California and never have to stop for a red light. When Eisenhower was elected he harkened back to the need for a "defense highway system" and immediately asked for funds from Congress to start the Interstate System. It was not foreseen, except by the homebuilders, that the "truckers' rights-of-way would soon be crowded with one commuter per car. Eventually, the system provided 58,000 miles of signal-free driving except around major cities, especially during "rush" hours.

Another major factor that set the stage for today's urban growth problems was the proliferation of suburban governments designed partially to prevent the central city from expanding its boundaries and imposing city taxes. Other suburban goals were exclusivity to create barriers to racial integration and the desire to operate their own local government for their own purposes.

Rural and anti-city state legislatures made the process of starting a new municipality easy and granted each of them the powers of land use and building controls as well as to have their own local police and fire departments. They also had no reason to be concerned with conditions in the central city as long as they didn't interfere with their agenda.

Even before the impetus of super highways and super subdivisions, the leaders of American cities took great pride in their unfettered growth. New York City, in the early 1900s, was the scene of the race to build the world's tallest building. Some even added spires and vertical ornaments to stay in the race. In the 21st Century, Asian and Middle East Potentates vie for the same titles. Psychologists believe that male hormones are at work on these projects.

Because only a few American cities had any form of Master Plan, most growth occurred at the whim of a landowner, a company wanting a signature building, or merchants creating larger stores to attract shoppers. Only Philadelphia, Washington, DC, and Salt Lake City had formal plans for their beginnings. The typical driving force was the attainment of wealth through banking, building, manufacturing plants, forestry, or transportation.

Although the titans of American business were dragged to Europe to experience its great cities, it seemed to have little effect on what was built at home. Of course, the great cities of Europe were mostly sponsored by Royalty that controlled both land and the public purse. America was, and still is, mainly a free-for-all for private enterprise to decide what it wants, how it will make money, where they can borrow the funds, and how fast it can be erected.

Public agency plans and controls are essentially reactive, superficial, and subject to market forces with the exception of the most sophisticated redevelopment projects or specific governmental projects. City governments were chartered to keep the peace, prevent the worst, finance utility systems, and maintain streets. Later, the management of social support systems was added.

As a result, every American city has some elegant neighborhoods, dangerous neighborhoods, some very attractive places to eat and shop, and miles of commercial strips where the worst of individual commercial development has been permitted. Many of those streets were part of the earliest routes between cities that simply got paved, then attracted gas stations and motels. Later, the invasion of the fast food empires and hold-up prone convenience stores added insult to injury. Unfortunately, the public streets surrounding old and new buildings were laid out, not for providing transportation routes, but to provide for pedestrian access, delivery of goods, and removal of garbage. When the horseless carriage arrived and Ford made them cheap, the city streets were deluged with both horse manure and honking flivvers.

As the cities expanded, architects and engineers proposed grand avenues, a la Paris, that brought prestige to its new neighbors. However, most urban centers are still plagued with the tight grids that cannot accommodate 21st Century vehicular demands. This seems not to have prevented massive new buildings designed to make the most of "location," no matter the inherent congestion.

It was not until 1926 that the concept of public controls about what could be built where was approved by the U.S. Supreme Court, upholding a lower court decision that a municipality, in this case Euclid, OH, could adopt a community-wide set of regulations setting zones for different land uses.

In keeping with the positive expansiveness of the American spirit, personal energy and financial desire drove the building of offices, homes, apartments, more roads, and more bank deposits. Every new development was cheered as a sign of progress. In fact, such a tumult of business activity created jobs by the millions.

Leading the "bigger is better" parade were retail merchants, land-owners, bankers, engineers, and contractors under the banner of the Chamber of Commerce. It should be noted that no community has been discovered to have a Chamber of Community Quality.

Rarely did any citizen or professional ask whether continued expansion of cities and towns was actually a good idea. Although the NIMBY factor is alive and well (Not in my Backyard!), few ever proposed or fought for "Not in my Community!" That is, until the retail giant, WalMart started pushing into small towns or urban neighborhoods where residents had the sense to value the products and services of their local merchants.

Even more rarely did any politicians ask for a cost/benefit study to determine whether an annexation should go forward or another 500 home subdivision was a good idea from a financial point of view. It did, however, dawn on some elected officials that each new home under $500,000 or so, could not carry its share of the cost of new schools, firehouses, parks, or road widening. Hence, the invention of the "impact fee."

This fee is paid by the builders of homes, apartments, condos, and commercial/industrial buildings based on value or square footage, and the collection of such fees are utilized to pay for the newly required facilities.

A more advanced method of passive control of community development, called "concurrence," is the concept that requires larger scale developers either to pay directly the cost of road and other community needs or contribute into a fund to pay for such facilities before he can receive final approval for his development.

In both of these cases, the developer/builder simply passes on such upfront levies to the buyers. This also results in making new housing less affordable to many valuable workers in the community.

Overall, local governments have invented many methods to help the community avoid being drowned by the public costs of ever-expanding development, but limited demands to halt sprawl have not been heard. Such objectors might be accused of being "un-American" in the manner that President George Bush labeled objectors to his war as defeatists or aiding the enemy.

The builders' and bankers' lobbies have fought any plans to have them pay for the public costs of growth. They have also resisted any responsibilities to provide affordable or workforce housing during the great development boom of the 1990s and early 2000s.

Reason has prevailed regarding the absolute necessity of thinking, planning, and deciding at a metropolitan scale when the systems under consideration must naturally flow through many jurisdictions. Even the rarely unimaginative Federal and State governments have seen the wisdom of overall planning for highways, water management, waste water treatment, and air pollution. Not to deal with these crucial practical and environmental issues was found to be nearly impossible.

Almost every major metropolitan area has some form of Regional Planning Council (advisory), Council of Governments (talkfests), or Metropolitan Planning Organization (required by Federal law for highway and environmental coordination). Most such efforts are heavy into data collection, holding conferences, and publishing reports with regional maps. Such entities usually have representatives from each political entity in the region. The task of each member is to guard the interests of his jurisdiction. Some such regional planning boards actually offer consulting services in fine grain matters, such as the New Urbanism while avoiding dealing with the tougher issues of sprawl.

Because there are no financial incentives to either the central city or the suburban communities to tackle true cross boundaries such as the social conditions in the inner city or the true costs of sprawl being allowed by the suburban communities, there is rarely an agenda for such matters. There are some outstanding exceptions to such narrow thinking.

Indianapolis, IN swallowed its parent county in 1970. It led to a City-County Council encouraged by the business community, the big city Mayor, the Governor, and the Republican State legislature.

Jacksonville, FL merged with its surrounding county toward improvement in schools, property renewal, unified utility construction, and land use planning. Although it is real metropolitan government, it has failed to control sprawl in the adjacent counties.

Louisville, KY consolidated with its County and is now governed by a County-wide Mayor and a 26-member council.

Miami-Dade County, FL created a two-tiered government in 1957. When further problems arose, a true area-wide government was approved that performs many municipal type functions but left the cities to perform limited activities.

Portland, OR is the only directly elected regional government in the United States, serving twenty-four cities and three counties. It primary mission is to manage growth through land use and transportation planning. The Regional government established an Urban Growth Boundary as a matter of policy combined with purchase of major open spaces. More information on Portland follows.

Before former Vice President Al Gore became the Nation's leader warning against Global Warming and Climate Change, he pinpointed sprawl as America's number one enemy. After concerns about militant Fundamental Islamics and out-of-control illegal immigration, the uncontrolled expansion of American cities, gobbling up the countryside to meet housing needs, is a long-term but serious threat to the health and welfare of millions of city/suburban dwellers.

In his bold, fearless book, *Sprawl Kills,* Joel S. Hirschorn, Ph.D., dissects and explains the powerful force and the human and financial costs of sprawl. Based on his background as chief scientist for the non-partisan National Governors' Association, he points out that "After 50 years of American housing and cultural being dominated by sprawl, millions of Citizens do not know of any other style of living.

"Sprawl kills is not a cute metaphor. It is a fact. Sprawl actually does kill, it makes people fat, tired, depressed, stressed, more likely to die in auto accidents and succumb to very serious diseases!" He continues, "Most people do not recognize the impacts of the built environment on the quality of their lives."

At a SmartGrowth conference in Kentucky, pro-sprawl advocates filled the front row with followers holding flags of the former Soviet Union. They portrayed SmartGrowth (a design concept urging mixed uses, calmed streets, small town squares, etc) as a socialist or communist plot, asserting, "unless you like the way Moscow looks and works, you should celebrate American-style urban sprawl!"

There is no question that slowing or changing the direction of the institution of continued sprawl will take high-level leadership, new Federal policies, State level vision, and community champions to buck the Chambers of Commerce and popular discussions on the national media. Rather than relying on the goodwill of the beneficiaries of sprawl, other motives for change must be found. At the top of the list of levers for redirection will be a new form of financial incentives that will hit communities in the pocketbook. That will get their attention.

Observation
A Glimpse of the Future

This author was ten when his parents took him to see "A Century of Progress", the 1933 World's Fair on the shores of Lake Michigan in Chicago. This city, famed for its stockyards and gangsters, had built a previous exposition in 1893 called the Columbian Exhibition. To justify the title for the 1933 showcase, its subtitle was 1833–1933.

The Century of Progress was dubbed the "Rainbow City," in contrast with the previous fair that was known as the "White City." The purpose of the fairs was to attract and impress visitors with the wonders of science and engineering, the fun of the Midway, and the tempting terpsichore of Sally Rand in her body stocking gracefully hidden behind her feathered fans.

In building after building were inventions, glimpses into the future, and wonders that would never cease. When the German dirigible, the 776 foot Graf Zeppelin, came to hover over the fair's crowds, the emotions were mixed due to the gigantic swastika on its rudder. Even in 1933, fears of Hitler's Germany crept into the minds of viewers.

In my ten-year old mind, it was a grand spectacle like nothing the imagination could dream up. With no television or picture magazines, one had to visit such a place to believe it. In the two years it was open, the exhibition welcomed over 39 million paid admissions, in a country of only 123 million.

One wonders how sensitive adults felt after leaving the "Century of Progress" with its grandiose structures and impressive avenues only to return to their real city. Only dreamers and architects probably mulled the question, "Why do our cities look like they do?" Because this question occurred to me in 1945, I chose the profession of City planning.

Observation
The Anatomy of Urban Stress

A million years ago, Ako, the caveman, peered down into the valley only to see Gufo the Bufo trudging up the hill toward Ako's cave. Gufo was much larger than Ako and his club was larger, too. Ako glanced back into his cave to check on his sleeping woman, his son, and his daughter. He also remembered the newly slain deer he had hanging from a rock.

As his mind and body registered fear and apprehension, as well as indecision, he was overwhelmed by conflicting emotions, to fight or flee. Although he had no idea of what was happening to him, Ako was stressed out of his grizzled gourd.

And so, today, experts tell us that modern men and women, afflicted by anxieties, exhaustion, frustrations, overwork, confusion, and fears are faced with the same emotions as Ako. The most common causes are conflicts at work and aches and pains, difficult family events, rush hour traffic, and economic pressures, all often beyond one's own control.

The accepted medical results of continuing stress are heart disease, clogged arteries, high cholesterol, strokes, susceptibility to infection, weight gain, diabetes, depression, erectile dysfunction, and a host of other maladies.

The personal and economic costs inflicted on large populations of stressed-out urban dwellers have not been measured. However, it is not difficult to imagine that the larger the city, the greater suffering from the impact of emotional stress. Long commutes, traffic congestion, street crime, and high costs of many essential items are experienced especially in the largest of cities. If one could have the amenities and cultural joys of the larger city with the pace and convenience of a smaller one, it might not be a bad place to live.

Observation
Silicon Valley Workers Get Googled to the Office

Employees at Google, Inc., in Mountain View, CA, get free food, game courts, and lap pools, but the best perk of all is a private chauffeured bus line that shuttles them from home to work and back. An article by Miguel Helft in the March 10, 2006 New York Times, reported that the company is running a 32-bus line all over the San Francisco Bay Area to make it easier for their employees to get to work. How it gets through the choking traffic is not explained.

The Company says that they are running a municipal bus line, except it covers several counties and many cities. Twelve-hundred workers take advantage of the free system. That's like sending your kids to a private school. The Bay Area Transit system, called BART, is beautiful and clean but runs only 104 miles and not to Mountain View. The better news is that the Google line runs on biodiesel and maybe a thousand cars stay home in their garages. Google is to be admired for its inventiveness, but it's a sad day for truly public transit.

Observation

Mayor Bloomberg Proposes to Make Nyc Green and he's not even Irish!

Billionaire Bloomberg, a very progressive Republican, on April 23, 2007, released a flock of green pigeons this day, each with a multi-million-dollar price tag dangling around its neck! All 127 birds represent the magnificent menu totaling in the Billions with an ambitious eye on the future. His MegaCity, the nation's largest, will continue to grow but be dedicated to reducing greenhouse gases.

He compared his blockbuster Plan with the 1850's first blueprints for Central Park or the construction of Rockefeller Center during the Great Depression. His quarter-century plan is to create "the first environmentally sustainable 21st-century city."

His admirable list of actions include platforms over rail yards and highways to create land for housing (and a million more people), opening 290 school yards for playgrounds, reduction of sales tax on hybrid vehicles, more bike paths, and nicer drivers.

His most controversial proposal, one which he previously opposed, is to launch a pilot program to create a tax cordon around parts of Manhattan and charge cars $8/day and $21/day for trucks who enter the zone. London and Singapore have successfully used this system to reduce congestion and build a fund for better public transit. He also promises to plant a million trees over the next year. Here's three million cheers for the Bloomberg Plan!

Chapter 3.
Curing Urbanitis in the Inner City

It is no secret that almost every American metropolitan area has a central city with a significant number of neighborhoods that house mainly poor Black people. However, such areas are not on the bus tour of the City, nor are they friendly places to walk in at night. Chances are, elder residents often don't leave their homes for fear of street gangs, drive-by shootings, and hustlers and prostitutes.

Over the last fifty years, everyone who could, fled the neighborhood leaving behind the poor, the infirm, the dope-heads, and the bad folks who prey on the weak. Left behind mainly are single mothers with children who lack the education, skills, or the possibility of rising in the society and economy.

The residents who have stayed may own an older home and fear the difficulties of moving into an unfamiliar community. Or they may be lucky to have a unit in a public housing project, or a Section voucher that allows them to rent private apartments in fair condition.

However, the neighborhood is dominated by young Black males who are most likely unemployed, on welfare, and/or are involved in illegal activities with a concentration in trafficking in drugs. Gang warfare, especially between Blacks and Latinos, is a growing problem across the nation.

Since the Roosevelt New Deal of the late 1930s, many programs have been created to improve housing for low-income families. Most of them have either suffered from national political sniping or been victims of unexpected changes in the demographics of American society or been caught up in the complexities of inner city politics.

Most large American center cities are hemmed in by historic boundaries or totally surrounded by newer suburban governments with no reason to deal with the concentrations of minorities in their center city. In some cities, the flourishing central business district with its gleaming bank towers is totally surrounded by problem neighborhoods.

In his frank and analytical book, *Inside Game, Outside Game*, David Rusk, former mayor of Albuquerque, NM, and a learned lecturer and consultant to cities and metropolitan areas, presents a telling description of why such troubled neighborhoods are growing and becoming a greater threat to the health of their regions. He reiterates the conclusion that unless the problems of the center cities are approached on a regional basis there is the likelihood that the next fifty years will be worse than the last.

Among his reasons are that the poor and working poor will be increasingly isolated from new employment growth in outlying areas and the costs of transportation will continue to increase. It is predicted that the center city's tax base will shrink, leaving it less capable of solving its internal problems. Although the bi-partisan mayors of major cities often unite in their appeal for more Federal funds, Congress usually turns a deaf ear.

The United States is the only developed country in the world that does not have a sufficient program of "social housing," meaning a decent dwelling for all its citizens. That condition probably is a reflection of inherent prejudices against Southern Blacks who moved to the cities for job opportunities and our less than empathetic feelings for the poor who are seen as lazy or unwilling to participate in our robust economy.

Historically, the churches created homes for the poor. That supply disappeared after World War II. We do have a menu of welfare programs including aid to dependent children and disabled individuals, Medicaid, and Food Stamps to feed the hungry.

The New Deal-inspired Public Housing program was similar to the European model in that decent housing would be built and rented to elders or young families just starting in life and working toward affording their own apartment or home. Some 500,000 units were built, and Uncle Sam provided financing and met operating deficits inherently due to intentionally low rents. High-rise elevator towers were originally meant for older folks without children.

However, after World War II, legions of Southern Blacks moved north searching for a job and a better life. As they moved into the most decrepit neighborhoods and into public housing, Whites left. The local Public Housing Authorities made the drastic mistake of allowing families into those elevator building, often with balconies, that became a nightmare for residents and management alike. After several decades, a few new non-profit housing companies emerged. The Ford Foudation named theirs LISC. James Rouse is among the leaders who, in retirement, created the Enterprise Foundation and NeighborWorks, partially funded by Congress that helps local non-profits to carry out their plans.

All these efforts are a drop in the bucket compared to the actual need for "Social Housing" in America. To make matters worse, land and construction costs as well as local governmental fees now make it almost impossible to build housing for low or middle-income people. In many communities, important service workers, teachers, police and firefighters, and government workers cannot afford to buy new homes even with two paychecks.

Following in the enlightened footsteps of Montgomery County, MD, many communities are attempting to introduce "inclusionary zoning" that requires developers to make provisions for some percentage of new units to be "affordable" or for "Workforce" housing. Its success has yet to be determined.

The so-called NIMBY factor (Not in my backyard) has been a major deterrent to the building of affordable housing. That exclusionary attitude is partially understandable because a person's home is the largest investment they are likely to make in his/her lifetime, especially in the face of rising home-owners' insurance, property taxes, and maintenance costs. Any new factor that might threaten that investment, no matter how liberal the individual may be, is to be avoided.

As David Rusk spells out in his book, the only eventually successful effort to move the people out of the worst neighborhood, and rebuild it, will be to counsel, train, educate, and employ those citizens, over a period of years, to the point that they can be absorbed, racially and culturally, into the mainstream of suburban or affordable urban life.

After examining over 50 metropolitan areas, and studying their demographics and cultural conditions, his strongly held conclusion is that this monumentally humane task can only be undertaken by the whole metropolitan population with its vast human and financial resources. He believes that no center city can be equipped psychologically, politically, or financially to undertake this enormous but absolutely critical campaign. That, in turn, presupposes that the leaders of both the center city and the multitude of suburban communities have the intellect and good will to rise above purely local biases and turf mentalities to think and act together.

The job of erasing the pain, despair, and the marginal existence of living in the worst neighborhood is only one of two lofty goals for our metropolitan cities.

The vital "Missing Link" is what we have labeled "Holistic Caring." This humane concept embraces three key factors:

1. Recognition and acceptance by the general population of cities that the people at the bottom of the society and economy do not choose to be there. Whatever the thousands of reasons they are there, deep down, no matter how they act or what they say, they wish they could see and find the way up and out.

No doubt there are people whose mental and physical health is so destroyed that there is little likelihood they could recover to live a normal life. However, the vast majority, whether they are prostitutes, drug-pushers, thieves, addicts, or gang members, are all doing what they do for money, money for food, shelter, dope, alcohol, doctors, pimps, cars, debts, family members, or whatever their survival demands.

2. American society is a reactive society. Each community, neighborhood, family, or individual naturally wants to pursue its or his goals and is only willing to participate in broader activities if there is a common threat or a process that requires a limited action. Going to war or electing a president are two of the most pressing national causes. Getting involved in local government stirs only a small portion of the general population.

If poor Black people are living in poverty or in a rough neighborhood, unless the non-poor, non-Black person or family is threatened, that's not their problem, especially if they're not in his town. Some small percentage of the general population will make an effort to relieve the negative conditions through their churches or philanthropic efforts.

A larger moral issue is whether a typical middle-class family has any sense of guilt knowing that dangerous and undesirable neighborhoods exist in their city or metropolitan area. Probably not. There seems to be no national shame about slavery or racial segregation in both the North and the South compared to the way Germany and Japan were ashamed by allowing their nation's governments to commit global atrocities.

To be fair, if the pragmatic Americans are offered a practical choice with a realistic mechanism and affordable budget, they would vote to help the people at the bottom. They can only do that if national leaders have an opportunity to reach for such goals as are proposed in this book.

3. The vast majority of urban redevelopment projects being undertaken by municipal authorities are with limited community development skills and heavily involved in the dynamics of Black politics. Many center cities are losing population because people have given up on whether any real progress will ever be made.

From time-to-time, a small, new, mixed-use project springs up or mixed income housing is built. But seldom is the renewal large enough or fast enough to turn around the vacant properties, the crime, or the reputation of the neighborhood. Local community development corporations are hand fed but seldom make much of a difference.

Two major efforts in Baltimore are experiments in community renewal. They are quite different in scope, approach, and the availability of resources. But both are important as national models because of their pioneering efforts and the fact that social and economic progress is being measured and reported on with amazing transparency.

James Rouse believed that peoples' lives could be improved if they were offered a better and safer environment. That philosophy was the driving force in planning and buildings Columbia, MD, over three decades, and it was his motive, after retiring from the Rouse Company, in starting the Enterprise Foundation with a million dollars of his own money.

Although its central theme was a decent home in a safe neighborhood, its underlying assumption was that individuals and families needed to be helped holistically not just with affordable bricks and mortar. That meant health care, education, financial support, individual and group counseling, and continuing guidance in finding a way up and out of the bad neighborhood.

After assisting dozens of cities create and finance affordable housing, the Foundation identified probably the worst neighborhood in Baltimore to launch the experiment of treating the causes of urban misery across a broad front. Sandtown-Winchester was a ninety-two-acre neighborhood, where 72% of the row houses were over forty years old in 1990, 29% of the units were vacant and/or abandoned, with a resident population of 3,200 people.

The concept was to pull together all the public, private, and non-profit parties with a stake in the area and to coordinate the many support and regulating systems working in the neighborhood, including social agencies, the school system, the police, parole officers, the churches (over fifty in the neighborhood), financing sources, housing experts, employment agencies, and anyone else who could be called on to help.

Because of its expertise in financing and building affordable homes, much energy was spent in acquiring sites and erecting new residential units in the belief that improving the physical environment and assisting residents into home ownership would be an important lift to the community.

The Enterprise Foundation has been steadfast in providing external leadership, and funding in the Sandtown-Winchester neighborhood has been successful in getting agencies to cooperate and to encourage churches to sponsor a wide variety of social programs to assist the poorest in the neighborhood.

Special praise has been given to the New Song Ministries and a local Community Development Corporation for struggling with the problems for over a decade. Those efforts include job training, talent development, a learning center, day care, after-school programs, and operating its own public school. Family health services such as primary care for all ages, health promotion, and education and immunization drives have been successful. These efforts, combined with a full spectrum of housing guidance and assistance have greatly improved life in the neighborhood.

However, it is still felt that many people with deep personal and behavioral problems have not been touched. Bart Harvey, head of the Enterprise efforts, indicates that the two greatest disappointments in the thirteen-year campaign have been the lack of jobs for unskilled workers and a shortage of community leaders with the time, energy, and abilities to spend the long, hard days, nights, months, and years of selfless dedication needed to make real progress.

East Baltimore has another bolder, broader action plan for the thirty acres of slums around the Johns Hopkins Hospital and Medical School campus. This plan includes building a two-million square-foot Biotech center adjacent to the world-class health care complex. Although Baltimore's Inner Harbor's waterfront condos are booming and gentrification of the closest neighborhoods is rapid, the "Outer Harbor," where the Black folks live, is still a shame to the City.

The major difference between the housing-social-services model of Sandtown-Winchester and the East Baltimore Development projects is that the latter is driven by powerful economics. It promises about 5,000 jobs, 1,200 units of mixed-income housing, and new retail space.

Fifty-six percent of the houses in the neighborhood are vacant and only 22% are owner-occupied. Over 700 of the 800 core residents live in poverty, and 85% of the families are headed by a single parent. Hopkins is expected to spend $1.0 billion and is the nation's number one recipient of federal research grants. The overall redevelopment team is dedicated to exemplary family strengthening, broad case management for families in crisis, and Family Advocates to assist in the relocation process. In many ways, the East Baltimore plan is a model of a business or institution with the most to gain taking leadership and funding responsibilities working side by side with the City and private foundations. Every inner city should be so lucky!

Another big city model is New York's Harlem Project. The neighborhood was famed for its Black musical and cultural history, but it suffered with deep poverty over several generations. Its location in the City has in recent years brought limited gentrification and investments. But, most importantly, it is the home of a noble and ambitious effort to save young Black kids from having to follow in their parents' footsteps.

In the early 1990s, Harlem was drenched in cocaine, homelessness, and gun-driven crime. One small non-profit organization, headed by "an average do-gooder," named Geoffrey Canada, was working to uplift a few kids to prevent their ending up in prison or dead. As his $3 million budget was spread out to offer after-school activities and anti-violence training for teenagers, he was frustrated by lack of more funding. He kept a list of the kids who wanted in but for which there was no room.

As the waiting list grew rapidly, he sought answers as to how his concepts could be expanded. It became obvious that helping the kids without the ability to help the parents or the schools they attended was hopeless. He decided to branch out and selected a twenty-four block area as his domain. Thirty-four hundred children under eighteen lived in that area. He then raised limited funds to provide social and medical services to those children. He and his growing staff developed a network of parents and kids. They created a myriad of confidence-building and expectation-raising plans to which the children responded with miraculous levels of behavior and learning.

Canada himself was a poster child who grew up in a tough South Bronx, living through drinking, fighting, and smoking pot, but he stayed in school. Through a scholarship to Bowdoin College in Maine, he went on to get a degree in Education from Harvard. His goal was to prove that poor Black children from Harlem could grasp the opportunities of learning in an atmosphere of sensitivity, empathy, discipline, and a belief in the highest outcomes.

In recent years, he has attracted both national and international attention and large sources of funds, built his own school, greatly expanded his arena and the services that make a difference in the children's lives. It's now called the Harlem Children's Zone, a place where hope and achievement exist side-by-side. His budget now exceeds $24 million, he has a staff of almost 700, and he is leading an army of over 6,000 kids. For an in-depth look at this exciting model, see www.ccebos.org/nytimes.geoffreycanada.

Fortunately, there are bright spots in the war against poverty and the uplifting of young people born in dangerous neighborhoods. The United States of America will never be whole or rightfully proud until the nation unites in holistic caring for the people left at the bottom. To erase these inhuman conditions will require a massive infusion of professional management and the expenditure of public and private funds over several generations. It would be a better use of money compared to traveling to Mars.

Observation
Comments from the City of Angels

The man who wrote this spontaneous letter is a successful architect turned developer who has lived in Los Angeles all his life. These are his direct quotes:

> LA is at the brink of meltdown. Air quality once thought to be diminished by carbon emissions is now recognized as much more complex. Soot is a problem even here at the beach where we live. It accumulates on everything. Current studies are beginning to demonstrate the relationship of the inhaled particles that are absorbed in the bloodstream that cause many problems. I am not a "the sky is falling" person, but I see the soot on household surfaces and hear of scientific reports on serious consequences.
>
> The transportation network is at max. The public transportation system, regardless of recent improvements, still does not adequately connect the parts. Political battles based on racial fears have deep sized critical routes. Businesses fearing disruption have successfully convinced Federal legislators to prohibit funding for certain routes because of "potential methane" (recently overturned after twenty years).
>
> First, the freeways became jammed, then the surface arterials. Now, the residential side streets are inundated. It can take three hours to go twenty-five miles on the Pacific Coast Highway, and there is no way to widen it or create an alternative. Similar circumstances exist along major freeways that are now over capacity.
>
> Latinos and blacks, once cooperating in their struggle for a place in society, are now adversaries. Avenue 206 is a dividing line. Street homicides are increasing. Witnesses will not come forward. Recently, alleged witnesses have been gunned down in the street in full daylight. A relative small enclave in LA has thirty-eight gangs.

There are 90,000 homeless people in downtown LA. Hospitals have been caught dumping indigent patients on the streets, including a recent reported incident of dumping a paraplegic in a nightgown.

I have worked hard to create "workforce housing." This gets us a little above the Federal guidelines for "affordable housing." Can't do it! None of the subsidies add up to make it work. Land prices are simply too high. We are bidding on a four-acre site next to a hospital (the third largest employer in LA) and we will not likely get it at $10 million per acre!

Don't get me started. Warmest regards, DO

Observation
THE GREATER ST. LOUIS BLUES

The Census version of the Greater St. Louis MSA consists of the totally independent City of St. Louis, its surrounding St. Louis County, six more Missouri counties and five Counties in Illinois. As the eighteenth largest metropolitan area, its population is about 2.8 million. As is so common, it has a Metro Commission with a ten-man board to deal mainly with transportation issues. It also has a Metro Sewer district to build and maintain a comprehensive sanitary collection and treatment system.

But the blues come from the City of St. Louis public school system. Its ninety-three schools, serving 35,000 students, many of whom are poor or homeless, is distressed to the point that the State Board of Education has voted to take over the troubled school system. Highways, ports, and sewers are a metropolitan problem, but the center city schools are not!

The City School system is $25 million in debt and has had six superintendents in four years. The high school graduation rate is roughly 55%. No doubt these statistics have been compared with the suburban school systems but that wouldn't help the situation. The City is over 51% Black; over 25% of the total residents live at the poverty level, with the Black poverty level at over 34%.

St. Louis has a rich history and, no doubt, has a successful upper and middle class. But historic boundaries, like the center city's limits, have resulted in a severe conflict about who can or is willing to solve educational problems, provide family support, job training, affordable housing, and similar problems. The spreading out of responsibility for neighbors welfare is as important as coordinating traffic and connecting sewers.

Does St. Louis have a plan for a Metropolitan People District?

Chapter 4.
The Waves on the Horizon

Let's not worry about the really long-term "guesstimates" that the United State's population will double to 600 million by the end of this century. It's difficult enough to get average American citizens to become alarmed about short-term projections such as the Census Bureau's current estimate that the Country's population will reach 364 million in the next twenty-three years due to increased birth rates and massive *in-migration*.

Interpolating the latest Census projections results in the following:

Population in Millions

Metro area	2000	Projected 2030	increase
New York, Northern NJ, Long Island	18.7	21.5	2.8
Los Angeles, Long Beach, Glendale*	13.7	16.8	3.1
Chicago, Naperville, Joliet	9.4	9.9	.5
Philadelphia, Camden, Wilmington	5.8	6.1	.3
Dallas, Ft. Worth, Arlington*	5.8	7.9	2.1
Miami, Ft. Lauderdale, Palm Beach*	5.4	7.7	2.3
Houston, Sugarland, Baytown*	5.2	6.8	1.6
Washington, Arlington, Alexandria	5.2	5.8	.6
Atlanta, Sandy Springs, Marietta*	5.0	7.2	2.2
Detroit, Warren, Livonia	4.5	4.7	.2
Boston, Cambridge, Quincy	4.4	4.7	.3
San Francisco, Oakland, Fremont*	4.2	4.7	.5
Riverside, San Bernadino*	3.9	5.7	1.8
Phoenix, Scottsdale*	3.9	5.9	2.0
Seattle, Tacoma	3.2	3.7	.5
Totals	98	119	21

*Considered to be "Sunbelt Communities"

It should be noted that the 21 million allocated to the listed fifteen metros represents only 33% of the anticipated national growth. The remaining 64% or 43 million could be attracted to the remaining thirty-five metro areas, smaller cities, and rural communities.

This means that the Country will be adding the equivalent of Southeast Florida's three urban counties (Miami-Dade, Ft. Lauderdale-Broward and Palm Beach) every twenty-four months! The vast majority of the new dwelling units will be forced to connect to existing systems of water supply, sewage treatment, roads and schools, thereby adding to the regional deficits in terms of traffic congestion, strained utility systems, and overcrowded schools.

The above chart is only for the fifteen largest metro areas. It forecasts that four of the next six areas after New York, Los Angeles, and Chicago, will each add over two million in the next twenty-three years. Each of the next thirty-five smaller metro areas will be called upon to absorb an average of 1.2 million over the same period.

A population of 1.2 million people will need 545,000 new dwelling units, will be flushing 1.1 million new toilets, standing under 800,000 new showers and pushing the buttons on 545,000 new garbage disposals. That will be quite a load on the existing water, sewer, and drainage systems.

Because the forces creating sprawl are so powerful and generally beyond the control of local governments, no one local entity except a form of regional government can halt it. The basic forces are high birth rates and in-migration from the farms or foreign countries. National governments in large Asian nations have worked to lower birthrates for decades, with modest success. No Central American or Mexican government has been willing to take on the battle with the Catholic church and try to mandate serious birth controls.

The United States government has operated under ambivalent immigration policies and enforcement levels. As of this date, a so-called Comprehensive Immigration Plan dealing with the complex problem of illegal border-hopping Hispanics is being considered by a split Congress. No one familiar with the human and economic issues of this tsunami of eager workers believes that the impact on

U.S. cities will be lessened. In our mobile nation, an extended family can move without limits from one region to another. All they need is money for gasoline and food. Our cities have not yet actually faced or even started to plan for the flood.

School systems will be overloaded, older housing will be crowded, and the pressures will hasten the citizenship process so that the newly arrived can settle down and live their version of the American dream.

Not much has been made about the Asian invasion, except for all those Valedictorians, but the tsunami from the Far East is just on the horizon. The only feasible path for metropolitan leaders, faced with these demographic challenges, is to start thinking regionally on all issues, beyond transportation and water supply, including housing, education, social services, language training, religious tolerance and, especially, urban growth boundaries. To build an imaginary dike around thousands of square miles requires foresight, imagination, and courage. Those metropolitan areas that can muster those traits will be able to solve their urban problems. Those that can't will continue to suffer the pains of growth.

Observation
"Minorities" Now One-Third of U.S. Population

Half the children born today in America are Hispanic, Black, or Asian. In May 2007, the Census Bureau declared that the combined so-called minorities now constitute 100 million of the Nation's 300 million people. This year, babies of Mexican heritage represented over 50% of the births in New York City.

Demographers are pointing out that a new generation gap is brewing between an older white electorate, sixty and above and the more youth-dominated minorities whose social and economic needs will be overwhelming. The Baby Boom cohort, 75 million strong, will be the predominate leaders and wealth-holders for the coming decades.

It is already clear that school districts in the Sunbelt states that are supported by property taxes and State and Federal grants are going to be the hardest hit in the struggle to meet the demand for public education of the new populations. It seems unlikely that the courts will support depriving resident children of such services no matter what the local populace feels. It will be interesting to watch as to whether these disparate racial groups will ever coalesce.

Observation
Brown Water Surfing in La-La Land

If you want to get a quick tan go to one of the brown water beaches in Los Angeles. Those are the ones where runoff from streets and parking lots and an occasional blurp of toilet water gets flushed into the mix. The Southern California beaches are world renowned, yet some of the beaches are actually unhealthy. Rugged surfers douse themselves and their orifices with peroxide to prevent infection.

It is not as if the engineers and health officials are stupid or lazy, it's just that the nation's second most overcrowded city has too much stuff to contain and process. Most of the beaches in Los Angeles County still score an A or a B in dry weather, but the social life for the beach crowd is still important even if swimming is less than thrilling. A major complaint is that dog lovers don't clean up. (Dogs are not allowed on most Florida beaches.)

California is slated to attract another ten million or more over the next twenty-five years. All those flushing toilets may totally overwhelm the beach cleaners. Wouldn't it be better if five million went elsewhere?

Observation
When Did We Lose the War on Poverty? And Who Cares?

Just weeks after succeeding the assassinated Kennedy, President Johnson announced a war on poverty. In the spirit of that concern, the Congress approved Medicaid (direct payments for health care for low-income families), the creation of Headstart (Free pre-kindergarten children) and other welfare programs directed at relieving the pain and suffering due to a variety of causes of poverty.

Later programs such as Section 8 apartment rental assistance were enacted to provide decent housing for the marginally employed or disabled people. Community Development Block Grants to cities helped with housing, neighborhood improvements, and community centers that offered training, meals, and other services.

These programs have been squeezed by Republican administrations and, even in the Clinton era, a Welfare-to-Work law supposedly forced some recipients to get jobs. The Bush Administration's reliance on the capitalist economy to provide more jobs for low-income workers backfired and pushed more uneducated and minority workers back into the ranks of poverty.

If you have ever stood in line at a fast-food outlet and watched a young woman, making $7.50 an hour, take your order and cooperate with other workers to get your food in a hurry, consider why she doesn't smile. She probably has an 8th grade education, a small child parked with her mother, and takes three buses to get to work.

Poverty in America has many faces. In addition to center city Blacks, Latino farm workers are paid low wages when they can work, and innumerable rural areas, cluttered with mobile homes, house Whites with little chance for advancement in a high speed, competitive 21st Century America.

However, almost every old city in America has neighborhoods where dope trade, gang killings, unemployed youths, and grandmas afraid to come out at night are the predominate population. Unmarried mothers with too many kids are a large population with few prospects for gainful employment. Crime generated from the troubled center spreads to the glassy downtowns, marginal neighborhoods, and gathering places for young people. The percentage of city populations living below the poverty level is well over 25% in the twenty largest cities and 12% of all Americans. Thirty-six million citizens have no share in the American dream and little hope of reaching the lower reaches of the middle class. Those millions are adding another million poor fellows per year.

Most suburbanites have no connection with these hundreds of thousands of unfortunate souls unless they are seeking yard workers or part-time maids. Hotel beds are made by these same people. The least fortunate are the homeless in a society that lauds mini-mansions and $60,000 cars.

Experts in the field who work with agencies devoted to reducing the pain of poverty will say that, in general, there has been little positive change in the plight of the poor for over a generation. And yet, in the early parts of the 2008 national election only one candidate of the twenty-plus list of both parties' hopefuls has ever mentioned the word Poverty. Former Senator and prospective Vice President in 2004, John Edwards published a promising essay, titled "Ending Poverty in America."

One would think that several other candidates might mention the dangerous conditions that poverty causes and have some ideas. Most are pledging more police, cameras, and tougher sentencing, as if the prisons are not already overflowing. Until the problems of these center city breeding grounds are addressed in a positive, creative, and uplifting way, they will remain a blight on the urban landscape and a black mark on our collective consciences.

Observation
"Smart-Growth" A Positive Urban Design Tool

It's not right to call New Urbanism or SmartGrowth planning fads. They are actually good tools for reaching higher density family housing, walk-able distances for convenient commercial and community services, and keen designs for a more urban streetscape by subordinating parking. But, as they have found out in Washington Township, eight miles east of Trenton, NJ, they are not the holistic community planning processes essential in designing a large workable community.

This small Township, led by State planning officials and a non-profit promoter of the SmartGrowth concept, adopted the principles heralded by those leaders and now finds itself in a financial disaster that may only be solved by using that dreaded term, Eminent Domain, to buy the undeveloped property in the town to prevent more overcrowding.

Superficially, the town is the perfect scene of white picket fences, garages in the rear, easy walking to shops with a greenbelt to tie it all together. Their 400-acre Town Center designed according to State guidelines as a remedy for urban sprawl, is too successful, and its happy families are overrunning the available schools. The Township built a high school and expanded other schools. Obviously, those improvements are not enough to hold the new kids.

A worse crime against holistic new community planning was the failure to assure a balance between the demands of residential units versus the business and industrial tax base needed to carry the load. (See the Columbia Planning Process). The growing tax bills in Washington Township have forced many retirees and families without children to leave town.

Observation
A Mega City Downwind

Hong Kong is about the size of the City of Los Angeles with about seven million people. Since the transfer from British rule to Mainland China in 1997, officials have hesitated to criticize Beijing about anything. Tangling with the red tiger is a dangerous sport. But in a recent election for Chief Executive for Hong Kong the issue of air pollution became a hot topic.

The pro-China candidate was forced to face and admit that its air pollution had already reached health-threatening proportions mainly due to coal-fired power plants on the Chinese mainland. It is like a child complaining about his grumpy grandfather's smoking too much.

The head of the Hong Kong University's department of Community Medicine said that, "mortality from respiratory, cardiovascular and other diseases increase sharply during periods of high smog." Some of the clearest skies that Hong Kong residents had seen for months occurred in February when mainland factories closed for a week to celebrate the Chinese New Year.

Observation
Miami-Dade's Line in the Ground

In 1983, Dade County drew a line in the sand or in the topsoil depending where you were standing. It was a victory for the environmentalists and win-or-lose for landowners. Some properties straddled the line called the Urban Development Boundary. Now, a quarter century later, it is under attack. Owners on the outside, so-called farmers, are complaining about their lack of a financial windfall!

The southern section of the County is forty miles wide with the Biscayne National Park (the only underwater National park) with its glorious reefs on the east and, to the west, the Everglades National Park, a unique treasure of tropical life and history.

Responsible park officials and the director of the Audubon Society maintain that, "Maintaining the Urban Development Boundary is critical to the restoration of the Everglades, an $8 Billion, thirty-year project involving the Federal, State and local governments."

The County paid consultants $4 million to evaluate the impact of moving the boundary. They assumed that some 700,000 more people would move to the southern part of the County. Eventually, the consultants recommended that the line remain where it is for another twenty-five years. A former city manager of Miami Beach is Chair of the thirty-member advisory committee. He concluded, "The people are going to come. It's not a question of whether we manage the growth, but how." This overview is a good example of what many metropolitan areas will face when the time comes to draw the line.

Chapter 5.
Curing Urbanitis at the Regional Scale

Over 180 million Americans, both from the United States and below our Southern border, now reside, work, learn, and play in the top fifty metropolitan cities that were founded in earlier centuries. The founding fathers laid out states and then counties with no vision of which would grow in population and which would stay semi-rural for decades and even centuries. Central Cities were incorporated followed by the creation of smaller surrounding municipalities, each designed with its own taxing abilities.

On top of this multi-layered pyramid of governments, more than four levels of taxation were imposed, depending on what the upper layers of Federal and State governments allowed the lower layers to levy. Although mostly well intentioned, elected and appointed officials occasionally struggled to cooperate while fighting for their own turfs, under those conditions, there was seldom a basis for guaranteed cooperation.

Only in recent decades has legislation and potential funding required a somewhat integrated approach to planning and constructing highways, air and water pollution controls, and limited efforts to enforce protection of wetlands and other sensitive lands. To tackle the most serious problems of the central cities, their suburban cousins and contentious counties rarely find a common ground for enforceable regional solutions.

What's missing is the essential mechanism for required cooperation and coordination on the issues that are actually regional in impact but ignored by parochial views. It is likely that the territorial vista will remain the same unless there are powerful incentives to require metropolitan-based solutions including establishing ultimate growth boundaries that may straddle the arbitrary lines of several communities.

To transform the cities and their metropolitan areas, a methodology and financial incentive concept must be created to give impetus for regional thinking, planning, and action in return for an attractive funding mechanism aimed specifically at allocating money based on a broad approach to helping these critical population centers become the livable, safe, compassionate, and proud places they desire to be.

Further, to initiate a long-range diversion of a portion of the inevitable national population growth by planning and building entirely new MetroCities in largely undeveloped areas of the country that could attract growth and develop beyond commuting distance from the burgeoning urban centers.

The United States has the territory, the know-how, and the economic energy to launch eight to ten new MetroCities with potential populations of at least 500,000 over the next decade. Depending on the ultimate capacities of these new large communities, they could absorb over five million people over the next twenty years. These two major elements are totally complementary and one cannot succeed without the success of the other.

The metropolitan areas, through the major centers of business, education, population integration, and cultural values, have been financially starved while a vastly over-fed military machinery and a glamorous but dubious exploration of outer space has eaten up Federal financial resources. The budgets for Housing and Urban Development and other Federal assistance programs for urban centers are miniscule, reflecting congressional and the administrative disdain for the plight of central cities that are falling behind in livability, even as they grow.

The following descriptions of key concerns will provide guidelines for how, with highly selective funding, cities can transform themselves.

Regional and metropolitan area thinkers and planners usually only deal with physical systems such as transportation, air and water pollution and, possibly, better design of neighborhoods, sub-centers, and the preservation of open space. They are trained as city planners to deal with streets, residential developments, utilities, industrial parks, shopping centers, and the all-important field zoning. Others are focused on regional models to analyze many of the key factors in urban growth, especially traffic planning, water supply, waste water management, or solid waste disposal.

It should be noted that none of these systems include the all-important fields of education, health care, recreation, social services, changing demographics, or extensions of life expectancy. In a single metropolitan area, there may be from six to twenty independent school districts. There might be a regional health consortium to coordinate health care and ambulance services and a coordinating council to encourage the many police chiefs to share approaches to roaming gangs. However, each has a separate budget and reports to locally elected officials dedicated to other fields of public management other than area-wide cooperation and the pooling of resources.

For a metropolitan area or urbanized region to qualify for the major new funds envisioned in this approach to managing growth, the watchword will be "Holistic Caring." This will mean that loose cooperation, information-sharing, and coordination will be replaced with the use of joint action contracts or compacts between legal jurisdictions at all levels of governmental and non-profit activities. The following checklist is offered as a generalized description of what work needs to be done to achieve true and more meaningful public service.

■ The Social Systems: No city or area can become morally healthy or secure as long as large numbers of citizens and migrants are left to fend for themselves in our competitive society. Recruiting, testing, training, and educating those on the bottom rungs is by far the most important challenge and the best investment that society can make. New solutions, based on new attitudes and the acceptance of diversity, can be designed and funded to go a long way toward the common goals of equality and prosperity.

■ The Health Care System: Fortunately, there is now strong national support for some form of universal health care in America. To make the health care program work, it is likely that the utilization of hospitals and other facilities may have to be managed on a regional basis. Local communities need to participate in applying the best care that is available in their region for all its citizens.

■ The Housing Supply System: No society can achieve self-respect, secure neighborhoods, and decent housing without a full commitment to make available new or old housing for every segment of the population. There are nations without slums. The United States has given lip service to these goals, but in recent decades, it has cut back on programs aimed at housing even the working poor. Each region must decide for itself what it will take to eradicate poverty and the living conditions and behaviors it causes.

■ The Education Systems: The United States has fallen behind many countries in the quality and availability of meaningful and useful education for all segments of society. This condition is partially due to the limited sources of revenues that school districts and public colleges can utilize to raise teacher's salaries, reduce class sizes, and instigate many other reforms that are out there to be effectuated. There is no more important system that affects the future welfare of the Nation.

■ The Transportation Systems: Recent recognition as to the harmful effects of fossil fuels and the political climate of oil-producing countries seems to indicate a positive future for autos, trucks, and buses that use other, safer fuels. However, that improvement will not lessen traffic congestion that is getting worse in most large cities.

Various methods of transit improvement and penalties for too much reliance on the individual vehicles are now starting to be tried. Every Metropolitan area must develop an aggressive program of transportation reform. Freedom to travel is not freedom to destroy many positive aspects of living in a metropolitan area. Great leadership will be essential to manage this critical aspect of urban living.

■ The Sustainable Community: To be serious about improving the social, economic, and physical environment for the benefit of all residents and workers, a new level of understanding is essential to deal with the negative impacts of many of our habits of living. Starting with the reduction of air and water pollution, managing solid waste treatment, safeguarding the sources of food supplies, and the wasteful methods of construction, there are many fields to be reformed in the future. Conserving water is the most obvious challenge.

■ Conserving Energy: Burning coal, oil, or natural gas to create our vital demand for electricity is a flame that is fading. The use of solar, wind, wave, or nuclear power is the most civilized approach to manage this all-important task for the whole nation and the world. America should be leading this parade, not dragging its feet due to its political connections with Middle East countries or the oil industry. Individual metropolitan areas have the capacity to lead in tackling these problems if they can develop the will to do so.

■ Enhancing Cultural Richness: Many organizations should explore the possibilities of broadening cultural opportunities, the dignifying of diverse ethnicities, appreciation of local history, and the glories of the arts in whatever forms are chosen. Communities should not be deprived of extensive participation in the valued fullness of cultural expressions.

■ Saving Land: As Will Rogers once stated, "They ain't making any more of it!" The entire realm of Smart Growth, New Urbanism, and other intelligent guidelines for the design of mixed use communities with their highest priorities on walking, subordination of motor vehicles, higher density housing, the expansion of alternate methods of transportation, taxation methods to reduce housing cost, and many other totally sensible ideas should be embraced by local governments and business leaders.

Halting sprawl is of primary importance if Metropolitan areas are ever going to get control of inefficient systems, continuing costly extensions of utilities, the ever-widening of highways, and the ruination of the countryside. When builders see that their future projects are in redevelopment areas and that creativity can replace cookie-cutter subdivisions, progress in containing sprawl will have arrived.

None of the above all-important key requirements for rational urban growth will take place until the wisest and most selfless men and women step up and devote their abilities, status, and their time to creating workable organizations to produce regional arrangements, agreements, and compacts to take hold of those systems. Local elected officials are often limited by the narrow demands of their constituents. Business and academic leaders are freer to stand up, apply logic, spell out consequences, and promote methods that will benefit all. Congressional leaders have the rare opportunity to forge working relationships above the level of petty politics. State officials can be more than helpful if the Governor wants to join the parade toward the highest level of regional cooperation and leadership.

The basic logic of focusing on the importance of dealing with all the systems of the society simultaneously is that the proposed new funding mechanism will only become available when the regional leadership produces a multi-faceted plan on how it proposes to spend the newly identified funds. Unless the plan is convincing in terms of the attention that has been given to improving the interrelated systems, no funds will be granted.

All potential funding will be tied to the steps being taken to halt sprawl in order to assure that the metropolitan area is serious about controlling that dimension of growth, because it is unlikely that all the other areas of concern can be eventually solved until the outward spread of development comes to a halt. Once those steps are taken, then the governmental jurisdictions will have more incentive to think and act in a truly cooperative fashion.

Observation
Ford Names Queen of Green

The Ford Company's CEO has named a lady executive to be Ford's Senior Vice President for Sustainability, environment, and safety engineering. At first it looked as if Ford was green with envy after reading that Toyota surpassed GM in car sales in 2006.

The Ford CEO is now being praised (except in Detroit and the White House) for admitting that greenhouse gases are partially caused by auto engines. However, the lady he promoted recently testified against the Sierra Club's proposals for more efficient cars in terms of higher miles per gallon requirements.

Apparently, Ford has made a lot of promises in recent years about better mileage but then backed out and promised cars to run on other than gasoline. Neither panned out. Does it make you wonder if there is a green ford in your future?

Observation
The Avalanche of Green

Only five years ago, the concept of introducing or requiring energy saving materials or systems was a marginal idea whose time had not come. Presumably, because global warming and climate change have seeped into the psyches of business leaders, it is now all the rage to seek environmental badges of honor for building or converting real estate according to the newest measurements of reducing the carbon footprint or just plain saving money.

The Simon Company, the largest of shopping center developers and operators, now has a code of "greening" that will lead to significant savings in operating costs. At their scale, those are not small potatoes. Major global investors are on the bandwagon, too. Developers in Japan and the U.K. are way ahead of the U.S.

The E.P.A. has shown leadership through education and research. They point out, "that, for each dollar invested in a building's energy efficiency, it has the potential to raise its market value $2 to $3 a square foot." That kind of arithmetic makes sense in the market, so the avalanche rolls on.

Observation
An Answer to Congestion? - Pricing!

It started in Singapore. In that single layer government, city, state, and nation all rolled up into one, when their central business district got too crowded with vehicles, they threw a financial cordon around it. Under that system, every vehicle has a barcode and a debit card similar to certain U.S. toll roads.

Every time a vehicle crosses the line, the owner gets charged. It has done very well in that Far Eastern metropolis. The idea was adopted for central London in 2003 and recently the size of its toll zone has been doubled to a football shaped district about seven by three miles in size. It costs $15.00 per day to use its streets. To make it easier for low-income commuters, bus and train fares were reduced.

Already unpopular for his stand on the Iraq war, Prime Minister Blair raised the idea of a fee for using all the major roads in Britain and received almost two million email messages condemning the notion. Not surprisingly, the Bush administration included $130 million in its recent budget to promote "congestion pricing systems" on U.S. roads.

NYC Mayor Bloomberg indicated a great interest in such a system for Manhattan. However, politicians jumped in and snarled the negotiations worse than the traffic. The jury is still out to see if the Mayor can get his way even in his city. Oy!

All these ideas might be more acceptable if the law required that all revenues from such tolls would have to be spent on improving public transit.

Chapter 6.
Launching the New MetroCities

This second but vital part of the one-two punch aimed at transforming American cities calls for eight to ten totally new MetroCities, that is, new mid-sized cities at metropolitan scale but with a unified government and/or a development authority to ensure that the negative conditions of existing cities are not repeated.

It is understood that the actual strategy for acquiring sites for new MetroCities will be a major task fraught with difficulties of all types. The timing of studies, planning, and related activities will be contingent on the *Partnership* having significant control over most of the site. Naturally, the entire acquisition process will be dictated by the availability of property, public or private, and a host of financial, legal, and technical issues. On the assumption that once a suitable site is under control, the following planning and related issues will proceed.

Planning and building whole new cities will be no small task. And, like everything else in a robust democracy, there will be plenty of controversy both about the idea, the MetroCity locations, and whose "ox is being gored?" Owners of large and small investments in existing cities will fear potential loss of value as wonderfully better conditions at new locations promises a more attractive and safer place to live, work, and play.

Those people who would fear new competition are the very ones who may have moved to Suburbia and left the old city to fix itself. However, once the existing metropolitan area has the incentives and funds to upgrade and reform its problem areas and its regional leadership exercises the political and economic will to set the boundaries of growth, the opportunity to divert population growth away could become a welcome concept.

It should be recognized that even ten new MetroCities with an eventual total population of five million will only attract between five and ten percent of the growth projected over the next three to four decades. During the policy debates on this bold plan, the question might be raised as to whether they should be planned for a population of one million each if the actual national growth exceeds the Census Bureau's projections.

On the positive side, imagine the conceptual thinking that will have to go into just writing the development program or specifications for a unique family of new cities. A highly organized process will be necessary to help set the individual goals for each new community depending on its location, its terrain, its larger regional economy, its relationships to its closest metro areas, and the demographic picture of its likely population over a twenty-five-year development period and thereafter. The planners will have to stretch their minds to grapple with the hundreds of variables inherent in the structuring and phasing of such a large and complex undertaking. However, if we can send a man to the moon, we should be able to plan and build a city for 500,000 souls.

The first team sent to evaluate a potential site will be the "environmentalists." These experts will study and clarify the most valuable natural sets or liabilities the site offers. The factors would range from the issue of natural habitats to grand vistas and ancient forests or burial grounds to be honored and protected. Questions will be raised regarding the capacity of part of the site to actually produce food or other crops of eventual benefit to the community.

A simultaneous task will be to undertake a study of the people, groups, and institutions already existing in the area of the potential site in order to recognize their values, attitudes, and human resources.

The new term, "Holistic Caring," will be used to raise questions as to how each set of social and economic goals will relate to all the others. Only after the "script" is written and approved, will the planners, architects, engineers, contractors, and the physical development experts start their computers whirring with alternate forms and what the on-the-ground interrelationships might produce.

The Community Development Plan for the new MetroCity will have many requirements. For example, with a development period of from twenty to thirty years, infrastructure and building construction will be plotted and scheduled to assure that neighborhoods are completed, facilities built and operating, and larger centers built in phases so that the early residents are free from the traffic, noise, and mess of the ongoing construction. Schools, community centers, shops, business and industrial buildings, parks and playgrounds, model homes, and speculative housing inventories will be available for immediate use so that early residents will not have to wait as is common in many real estate ventures. In most cases, institutions have a "wait and see" attitude before committing to doing their share. A unified development effort will avoid that typical situation.

The new MetroCity will be planned to meet at least this short list of guidelines:

Land will be allocated based on the general formula that was used in Columbia, MD, which has stood the test of time for forty years and has produced a wide variety of living styles, a blend of natural and man-made beauty, an extremely well-served set of services and facilities, and a consumer and job-driven economy that is the envy of new communities. To be sure, Columbia is located in a high-growth corridor between two expanding metro areas, but its economic success is also due to the developer's aggressive efforts to attract a wide range of job-producing employers.

> To provide for the targeted 500,000 residents, approximately 225,000 dwelling units will, at an average residential density of seven units per acre, occupy about 30,000 acres or a little less than 50% of the land.

> The formula would allocate 25% or 16,000 acres of the land for parks, open spaces, farms, non-profit facilities, trails, campgrounds, lakes, and rivers.

> To create jobs and a healthy economic base and produce the equivalent of property taxes to help fund long-term community needs, 18% or 12,000 acres would be set aside for business, commerce, and appropriate industry.

Approximately 9% or 6,000 acres would be allocated for transportation systems including transit ways, parking facilities, roads and streets, equipment repair facilities, and transfer stations.

These acreages total <u>64,000 acres or 100 square miles,</u> coincidentally the same size established by George Washington and Thomas Jefferson for the new capital of the new country in 1790. The site straddled the Potomac River into both Maryland and Virginia. That ten-mile by ten-mile square held steady until 1836 when the Congress released the Virginia portion to Fairfax County.

Some observers may claim that the creation of new MetroCities will exacerbate the flight of Whites to the suburbs by giving them the opportunity to move to a new community far from the problems they originally moved to avoid. One of the goals of the new MetroCities will be its responsibility to provide a full range of housing, including housing for low-income workers. If the typical MetroCity is to achieve its residential build-out in thirty years, this would mean an annual production and sale or rent of over 7,000 units per year. Columbia's peak residential production, with twenty-seven builders at work, was 2,500 units per year.

Although the Community Development Plan would necessarily respond to the topography, natural features and special places, it might follow in the footsteps of England's largest new town, Milton Keynes, that was laid out in a grid. An American version of that configuration might use one-mile grids resulting in 100 sectors of 640 acres each. This fits into the national mapping system used in a substantial portion of the United States. The grid may end up with curves and angles to respond to the particular site.

An all-important planning goal is to subordinate the use of individual vehicles while providing and prioritizing the use of light rail, electric, or otherwise fueled buses, all-weather trams, taxis for the infirm, and walking and bike ways. Fossil-fueled trucks, cars and buses from the outside would be directed to transfer stations on the perimeter of the MetroCity where non-polluting vehicles would pick up the people or the goods for delivery into the new community. The major center of the MetroCity would have underground delivery facilities as has proven so successful at Orlando's Walt Disney World.

Housing developments will follow new concepts and standards of vehicular storage that will make the typical two-car garage unnecessary. Community-wide delivery services will make purchasing easy and personal trucks obsolete. A wide diversity of housing types will be encouraged to provide for new and changing family structures. The use of home businesses will be assisted by the installation of wireless systems and other technology as it becomes available.

Every neighborhood will have a variety of easy-to-reach, mixed-use commercial and community services within short walking distances including sidewalk cafes, bike repair shops, a price-controlled convenience store, a pre-school center, and other retail outlets. Dog walking areas will be nearby. Larger sub-centers serving several neighborhoods will assure competition among retailers. Small community storage facilities will be developed at convenient locations.

The new MetroCity will be designed to be totally free of man-made pollutants. Electricity could be obtained off the power grid or other sources of solar, wind, or other new forms of energy generation can be utilized and every effort will be made to make them work. Energy saving will be built into all homes and buildings, public area lighting, and appliances.

Every new MetroCity will be a "green" city. This will result in the use of recycled and non-destructive materials, the use of recycled water, the collection of rainwater, advanced methods of waste-water treatment and the collection and processing of solid wastes for uses in the community.

The new MetroCity will seek a wide range of cultural activities and facilities based on its size and magnetism. Visiting scholars, artists, and performers will be a regular fare with emphasis on creativity and leading-edge media.

The new MetroCity will promote and manage a broad program of health prevention, care and fitness that will be integral in the community, the schools and family life. A wide array of participatory sports will encouraged with first-rate facilities available to all those who live or work in the new community. Non-profit groups such as YMCAs or the Boys and Girls Clubs will be enlisted to organize and operate the programs.

The public school system will be the educational backbone of the new community. All opportunities to provide affordable education at all levels will be the highest priority. Every MetroCity will have one or more higher-level colleges or universities.

The design of neighborhoods will take heed of the possibilities of New Urbanism and SmartGrowth as they can best be applied. The emphasis will be on livability, security, maintainability, and person-to-person communications designed to have neighbors know and help each other. Every neighborhood will have a variety of housing types and prices as well as permanent, supported housing to assure diversity across the board. The use of Land Trusts may well be the best mechanism for assuring the long-term availability of affordable housing.

The new MetroCity will be planned to be built over a twenty- to thirty-year period. Its cellular growth will recognize that parts of any city become obsolete and will need refurbishing and/or rebuilding as they move along the life cycle. Repurchase mechanisms will be built into property deeds so that individual or other owners will not be able to unreasonably prevent rebuilding or recycling. Investments and market values will be honored.

The Community Development Plan will place importance on the essentiality of the best in urban design, architecture, and landscape design in the creation and construction of all pieces of the community. Public and private art making, teaching, integration, presentation, and marketing will also be most important in the growth and development of the maturing community

The Community Development Plan will be created by teams of urban designers, architects, engineers and artists brought in to deal with each of its components as well as their integration into the whole. Citizen participation at some level will be encouraged. Among the assignments will be the introduction of a visual theme or concept and the design of a proposed new MetroCity's physical focal point, to be unique to the single community. That focal point will become the visual brand of the new city.

The community planning process will be divided into phases starting with a feasibility phase, including site analysis, application of systems analyses, economic-market analysis, and overall financial analysis. If these studies produce a positive result, then preliminary physical planning will produce a sketch plan for ultimate development. This phase would take approximately twelve to eighteen months.

That sketch plan, the feasibility analyses, and appraisals will be shared with the public. Comments and questions will be dealt with prior to proceeding with land acquisition. At that time, work would start on preparing the Community Development Plan in five-, ten- and twenty-year phases. Each step of the way will be subject to testing it against the Financial Model and prevent the adoption of a non-feasible plan. Depending on potential difficulties in acquiring the site, this phase would also take twelve to eighteen months.

When the Community Development Plan is available for public comment and internal review, it will be open to questions and possibly revised. This phase will take approximately six months. When the Community Development Plan and the initial development and construction budgets are approved, detailed construction documents will be initiated.

On the assumption that the first phase of development will include dozens of different types of improvements, the task will be to control each of the pieces so that the community can open with sufficient facilities to allow the first residents to move into a functioning Community.

Prior to this initial construction period getting into full swing, a quick "mini-town" will be needed for on-site professionals such as officials, architects, engineers, contractors, inspectors, accountants, public safety officers, visiting press, and hundreds or thousands of workers.

It will have to provide housing, offices, clinics, stores, recreation facilities, vehicle repair shops, storage buildings and yards and water and sewage treatment plants, solid waste disposal, and other systems needed to operate this "temporary" builders' community for possibly twenty years. This community will need many of the same services required by any small town depending on what is available in the existing local area.

Under a design-build approach, a prototype, prefabricated set of construction systems will have been conceived, designed, and cost estimated during the feasibility stages of planning. Once the decision is made to proceed with the community, pre-selected contractors will be mobilized with a tight schedule toward getting these housing and related facilities in place and functioning within 90 to 120 days.

In the interim, buses, trucks, and helicopters will bring personnel and supplies into and out of the site depending on what facilities may exist in the area.

Based on previous experience, it is estimated that it will take from six to seven years from the time the new community is authorized to the point that people can open businesses, schools, offices, and clinics and move into homes and apartments.

This schedule assumes the full use of the expertise of medium to large contractors, major homebuilders, non-profit institutions with development experience and government agencies with similar capacity. Every possible use of minority contractors would be brought into the process. Emphasis would also be on the use of U.S. companies.

Advanced methods of scheduling, project control, and cost accounting would keep track of progress and focus on problems or delays. Labor disputes would be handled by experts in that field. In some cases, central purchasing would be used to assure deliveries and cut costs. A major financial management and accounting center would control the flow of funds, and in-house auditors would keep watchful eyes on those functions.

It is assumed that all functions of the new MetroCity development entities would be free of local and state zoning, subdivision regulations, permitting, and licensing since the overall initial owner-developer of the project would be an arm of the U.S. Government. Such flexibility would be essential in designing and building a new city. New codes would be prepared to protect the integrity of the larger community and rights and investments of property owners.

Depending on financing, if one new MetroCity were authorized every year for ten years, the last one would not start construction until the thirteenth year of the program and be finished, barring any catastrophes, in a forty- to forty-five-year span of time. This is consistent with the schedule of the British New Towns that took almost fifty years to complete, totally thirty-three small towns housing somewhat under two million people. However, if a faster schedule was required, more teams could be employed to reduce the development times.

Illustrative Budget for Launching a New MetroCity (In $ Millions)

Land acquisition and related costs	180
Planning, engineering, financial analyses	10
City-wide initial infrastructure	100
Residential land improvements (10,000 units)	400
Community facilities	80
Commercial/industrial land improvements	30
Utility systems	200
Total	1000

These funds would be expended over a five-year period. Revenues would start in the fourth year by selling finished residential parcels to private builders and non-profit housing organizations. Land sales would approximate $800 million in the fourth and fifth years. For the purposes of setting an illustrative marketing budget, rough calculations indicate that the sale of residential parcels over twenty-five years (after deducting 20% of residential land for supported housing), would produce approximately $18 Billion in gross revenues. Additional revenues from the sale or lease of business/industrial parcels would produce another $9 Billion. The eventual sale of various systems could produce additional revenues. Such calculations are presented in constant dollars and do not account for inflation.

The financial models will deal with all aspects involved in the building of the new MetroCity and typically would include all costs, revenues, charges, and reserves, based on actual and projected expenditures and revenues. Examples of this type of long-range real estate model are available through consultants who devised and operated them for many years.

One measure of the success of such a huge undertaking will be in its long-term feasibility with the recognition that recessions do occur and that problems do arise. However, since the overall financial strategy of such a building project is to purchase large areas of land at rural values and, over time, convert it to urban values, the final question could be, "How much money will it make?"

The real question will be, "How happy and broadly successful are the residents, their families, the thousands of employees, the businesses, and the leaders of the public systems?"

To achieve the financial goals of the public and private investments in the project, a massive, long-range professional marketing program will be necessary. It would be launched two years before initial occupancy was scheduled. The program would include the building of the first guest hotel and a state-of-the-art presentation-sales center to be built at a prominent location from which site tours would be generated. In that exhibition would be information on every aspect of living, working, retiring, teaching, or painting in the new MetroCity.

A regional, national, and international information program will be kicked off including a high quality web site with monthly updating, materials for mailing, a public relations campaign featuring prominent visitors, political leaders, school children, tourists, foreign visitors, and key people involved in the planning and development process.

Selective promotional efforts aimed at business and industry would reach investors, venture capital managers, real estate professionals, bankers, major retailers, specialized industry leaders, foreign companies, and any other audiences who might be interested in living or locating in the most advanced, clean, and green new metropolitan area in the U.S. The marketing budget, not including sales commissions, would probably be in the range of $25 to $30 million a year and be active for at least twenty years.

Observation
American Planner Takes on Global Communities

Peter Calthorpe, a Berkeley, California-based planner, one of the founders of the New Urbanism movement, is scattering his design concepts from Moscow to Aqaba to Albuquerque. Imagine the Russian capital with 7,400 acres of raw land near the Domodedova International Airport, twenty-two miles south of the Moscow Center. The project plan calls for 167,000 housing units, up to forty stories tall and with 32 million square feet of commercial space. No Communists in that team! Actually, the developer is from Dubai in partnership with a large "Russian firm."

Calthorpe admits that he and his fellow New Urbanists deal well with streetscapes but don't always fix on regional issues such as transit and essential employment. He recently was awarded a $100,000 prize by the Urban Land Institute, a non-profit educational and trade group.

Regional issues are not design assignments, they are political, societal, and economic. There are not many experts in those fields ready to help urban regions mature into metropolitan leadership.

Observation
China and India Have National Urban Growth Policies

Both of these burgeoning nations, with populations exceeding 1.3 Billion, have adopted policies that they back up with favorable financing. In China, Chongqing, already a metropolis of 12 million, has been chosen by the Central Government to absorb two million people in the next five years and repeat that in the next five.

The national goal is to move poor farmers to chosen cities, build high-rise towers to house them, and put them to work building a productive economy. Steering the growth away from Beijing, Shanghai, and other coastal cities, is part of the strategy. However, China is putting the human economy ahead of the environmental agenda. The skyline in Chongqing is already obscured most days of the year. On the good side, they are moving a gigantic belching steel works out of the urban scene into the farming countryside.

India has a similar strategy. They intend to divert 100 million people from moving to Delhi or Mumbai, already on the edge of a congestion and air-pollution disaster. One city chosen to vault its population from 2.5 million to 10 million plus is Nagpur, in the very center of the Country, 500 to 1,000 miles away from any other city. The government and private investors are pouring hundreds of millions into housing, shopping centers, schools, and an eco-friendly transit system to move the hordes about, years before they will likely afford a car. How lucky can they get?

The Indian government has pledged $29 Billion to sixty-two cities to upgrade their infrastructures, international airports, and factories. The plan includes exporting cars to the West at prices that will make Detroit and Toyota cry.

India especially has been investor friendly and China is learning the concept. They use public funds to prime the pump then open the opportunities for private enterprise to do its thing. Not a bad idea.

Observation
Bold Leader in Wind Power

One company with a history in coal, gas, and nuclear power has taken giant steps to make the most of nature's winds. The FPL Group, daddy of Florida's Florida Power and Light (known irreverently as Florida Plunder and Loot) has leapt to the head of the line in capturing the freest and cleanest source of energy.

After a corporate melt-down in recent years and taking advantage of Federal tax credits established to encourage alternative sources of power, it has constructed, in just a few years, 6,400 of those magnificent forty-story, long-armed giants that twirl 24/7 without puffing one ounce of bad stuff into the air. On fifty wind farms in fifteen States, it produces enough electricity to totally serve five cities each with a population of 500,000.

Imagine a new city of 500,000 totally powered by a wind farm on the nearby hilltops. Faster, cheaper, and more welcome than a nuclear generator, these mechanical monsters can turn for years without an overhaul. The Country welcomes new ideas (or did the Dutch invent them?) and the companies that put them to work.

Observation
Personal Rapid Transit...Coming Soon

PRT as it's known had been a hot idea for decades. It was part of the advanced planning for the new town of Columbia, MD, but it was scuttled when the Federal Government's transit granting agency chose the hilly college town of Morgantown, WV, as its pilot location. The most senior of US Senators, Robert Byrd, made sure his bailiwick won.

Considered a white elephant for many years after its 1975 opening, its costs had skyrocketed to $138 million. Initially designed to connect two campuses of West Virginia University, it is now part of the fabric of the entire city. To take it on its 3.6 mile route, you just enter a car that holds twenty-one people, press a button and the computer driven system cruises silently on rubber tires, propelled by electric motors. No other such system has been built.

But now, London's Heathrow airport is installing four-person pods running on an elevated track. Several American cities are now taking the concept seriously and may be bold enough to follow in the footsteps of the English system.

Observation
China's 21st Century Great Leap Forward

China is so vast and complex and organized so differently than the West, it is hard to tell who is speaking for whom unless it comes directly from President Hu's mouth. (Hu is President? Hu is President!)

Nevertheless, Ma Chengliang, the manager of the Dongtan project, announced that a new metropolis will be built in the District of Chongming on the outskirts of Shanghai. It is to be a true eco-city for an eventual population of 500,000 located in the middle of a vast wetland nature preserve.

The highly competent British firm, Arup, has a team working on all the criteria for the eco-city including the design in a small, light, non-carbon vehicle for personal transportation. They indicate, "Dongtan will be compact, inspired by traditional towns in which water plays an important part of life. Every building will have its own windmill and energy saving will become a model for China. The Chinese urban population is growing so fast that many new MetroCities will be necessary.

Observation
Capital of India...a Megacity Disaster

New Delhi was a planned capital worthy of a huge nation but something went wrong. A few of its grand boulevards are still regal as are the Victorian public building housing millions of bureaucrats. Calcutta was the center of British India but Delhi had been the capital of several ancient empires and was more centralized in the geography of the nation.

So the occupying army of King George V changed the capital with the flourish of a feathered ink pen. Then Edwin Lutyens, a noted English architect, was brought in to produce a plan for the New Delhi to be superimposed on the network of shrines and ancient cities. His plan is an explosion of grand boulevards, a la Paris, with gigantic traffic circles now jammed too full of horseless carriages and put-putting three-wheeled rickshaws.

When India gained independence in 1947, the enlarged New Delhi was named the National Capital Territory of Delhi. Though blessed with being more central, the climate of the region has damned the huge current population of 15 million to frigid winters due to cold fronts sweeping down from the Himalayan mountains and in the summer, stifling heat waves reminiscent of an African desert.

In the early years of the 20th century, 60% or nine million people lived in slums of shacks and abandoned buildings and endured inhumane suffering. As the Eastern cities have learned, the only way to house great hordes of humans on small parcels of land is by going up. Hong Kong, Singapore and the Emirates have learned these lessons.

So, a new Master Plan has been approved toward housing the next eight million due to arrive in New Delhi in the next fourteen years. The Plan authorizes the demolition of whole neighborhoods currently occupied by over three million to be cleared and covered with high-rise towers. One doesn't know who to sympathize with more, the slum-dwellers or the politicians who have to enforce the Plan.

Chapter 7.
A Public-Private Partnership To Lead the Way

When the United States Government pledged to build a super bomb toward ending World War II, it set up a top secret task force headed by one-star general, named it The Manhattan Project, set up an obscure base in the desert, recruited thousands of scientists, engineers, and other bright people and went to work. Many in the Congress did not know the project existed. It was run as a combination private company and field army. They got the job done and just in time.

In the face of Russia's early launch into space, President Kennedy declared that America would place the first man on the moon! Emergency budgets were set up, World-class professionals were mustered, including German scientists, a new space agency was set up, huge budgets were activated and, as promised, an American team was first to walk on the moon. The space agency was also run outside the typical constraints of a government agency.

American cities are not threatened by an external enemy but by an equally insidious enemy from within. Although Americans can take pride in the many wonderful museums and monuments, the glass and steel skylines and the glitzy magnetism of Times Square, they do not take visitors to other parts of their cities. Almost every American city has neighborhoods occupied by poor or marginally employed African-Americans or other minorities. Walking or even driving through such areas is not considered the safe thing to do.

At the same time, the visitors are not taken to see the outskirts of the region, the seemingly endless subdivisions and strip centers that stretch for miles. And certainly, no friend is taken on a tour of the freeways during the peak hours of commuting.

Slowly but surely, the rotting core of every center city, around the central business district, is creeping outward. As low priority housing and redevelopment programs move very slowly and unemployment is endemic for the lowest income people, the citizens of the region are not proud of those conditions but mainly choose to ignore them. As seemingly uncontrolled immigration continues, those new people will find beds to sleep in and shops that sell their ethnic foods. Landlords will respond in the only way they can.

Although the authorship of the saying, "Where there is a will, there is a way," is not known, most people believe that axiom. Another axiom is that many problems can't be solved by just "throwing money at them." That is also likely true. However, it is true that a will to accomplish a very difficult task grows if there are funds available to those who try. The following proposals are offered because there definitely needs to be the recognition of the problems and the broad national will to tackle them.

In some countries, only massive, destructive riots that result in loss of lives and property get results for urgent leadership and legislative action. Americans are slow to accept community problems preferring to live their own lives in peace and comfort. Riots and threats usually bring forth modest well-sounding palliatives but little long-term action.

As James Rouse said, "Cities are like they are because no one believes there are solutions and then acts to change them." That's why he conceived Columbia, MD, to show, in a small way, that man can create safe, open environments. Half the battle to generate the will to make our cities safe and open is to have a sufficient mechanism and potential funding in place with powerful and positive incentives to move forward.

The proposed organization, the *"National Partnership for MetroCities,"* to lead and implement bold plans for the repairs of our cities, the halting of urban sprawl, and the building of new MetroCities will have dual major functions to carry out its massive assignments. The same sense of urgency that applied to the atomic bomb and getting a man on the moon should apply to the state of our cities that takes a daily toll of suffering and deaths due to national ignorance or neglect.

Social workers, teachers, or police officers will share what they discover every day about what life is like in the worst of the neighborhoods. Obviously, people do not choose to live there or experience the grief due to shortage of funds, the threat of gangs waging wars over drug turfs, or because they are jobless and with few prospects. Any leadership group in any metropolitan area that decides to take a good hard look at the deep reality of those neighborhoods will be horrified.

American cities cannot continue to just grow outward and pave more daily escape routes to suburbia. Center city mayors and administrators cannot now look to suburban concern or assistance because there is no mechanism for them to work together except on transportation coordination, as demanded by Federal laws and regulations. City redevelopment agencies are unable to be aggressive because funding for such programs is miniscule and typically deals only with housing and not the real problems of center city neighborhood dwellers.

In 1965, the Congress created the Department of Housing and Urban Development, (HUD) "to provide assistance for housing and for the development of the Nation's communities...that will have a major effect on urban community and suburban development." Due to the practical abandonment of political concern for the state of the cities, HUD's annual funding has been whittled away to a total of $25 Billion that is distributed through the fifty states to hundreds of communities. Through a supposedly competitive process, small amounts go to winners, and losers get nothing. HUD has paid no attention to the larger metropolitan issues and continues to guarantee home mortgages in the sprawling suburbs.

In 1969, the Congress created the Environmental Protection Agency to "encourage productive and enjoyable harmony between man and his environment..." Further, the law stated, "The Congress... recognizes the profound impact of man's activities on the... natural environment, particularly the profound influences of population growth, high-density urbanization, industrial expansion... and recognizes further the critical importance of restoring and maintaining environmental quality to the overall welfare and development of man..."

EPA's budget of $8 Billion is mainly devoted to Clean Air, Global Climate Change, Clean Water, Land Preservation, Healthy Communities, and Environmental Stewardship. Its work is sometimes ignored, although often valued because it prevents the worst, tries to remedy disasters, and sets standards on pollution. Its plate is too full to expect it to deal directly with problems of the growth of cities.

These combined declarations of national policies and agency creation practically mirror the tenor of what new policies are urgently needed, but it is unlikely that either HUD or the EPA could be diverted from the many worthwhile programs they struggle to manage. Both agencies are under continuing attack by the conservative elements in the government dedicated to business and industry's rights to carry on their activities free from governmental interference.

America's jaundiced view of governmental agencies and their workers is prejudiced and unfair. The vast majority of public agency employees are dedicated, do their jobs, often under difficult circumstances, and care about bringing public service to the beneficiaries.

However, the highly complex and urgent nature of the combined approaches envisioned in the mission statement of the proposed *National Partnership for MetroCities* would be better served if its functions were carried out by an entity that needs to be aggressive, pro-active, business-like, and free from the heavy hands of Federal rules, regulations, and restrictions. It would operate more like a large foundation, carrying out its missions with prudence, energy, and the recognition that working at the *Partnership* would not be viewed as a place that emphasized retirement benefits over hard work.

It is proposed that the President sworn in on January 20, 2009 and the new Congress declare a state of deep national concern about the quality of life in American Cities and Metropolitan Areas. The Act creating *The National Partnership for MetroCities* would authorize a private, non-profit corporation in the national interest.

Its nine person Board of Directors, four to be appointed by the President and both Houses of Congress on a rotating basis, and five, a majority, to be appointed by the President, chosen as non-governmental members from a slate nominated by the top five national charitable foundations dedicated and active mainly in housing, urban development, and the health and welfare of American cities. The President would appoint the Chairman of the Board, and the Board would select the President/CEO of the Partnership.

The *National Partnership for MetroCities* would have several major functions:

To aid existing metropolitan areas:

1. To determine the fifty metropolitan cities which, due to deteriorating conditions in the central city and extensive suburban growth, would most benefit from higher levels of regional cooperation, unifying methods for attacking common social and economic problems and be granted Federal funding to improve the quality life in their areas. An important component in the mutual cooperation between federal, state, and local jurisdictions would be the establishment of urban growth boundaries and methods of enforcing them.

2. Once guidelines for participation were established, *Partnership* teams would develop relationships toward starting the process in each of the metropolitan areas. The teams' purposes would be to help and encourage successful application for funding under the guidelines. Swift administration of the evaluation and funding would be the watchword.

To the extent that financial advances would hasten the process, such an approach would be favorably viewed. Existing programs of positive city improvements in the lives of its residents or innovations toward halting suburban sprawl could be supplemented. The funding envisioned could eventually provide funds for all 50 of the regions, once qualified, to benefit from the program. Congress would be called on to attach conditions to existing subsidies to local governments to assure consistency with its new Urban Growth policies.

<u>To promote the new MetroCities:</u>
1. To develop a long-range plan for the development of eight to ten new MetroCities in areas to which demands for new growth could be diverted to aid in the relief of pressures to overbuild existing metropolitan areas. Once prospective regions have been identified, priorities would be set and land acquired for the initial new MetroCity.

2. The *Partnership* would create a long-range Community Development Plan for each MetroCity, describing the scope, extent, land use allocations, and major systems of community development and promulgate planning and development guidelines for all aspects of its future growth. In addition, budgets would be established and funding plans and schedules would be prepared.

3. To take over the responsibility for the actual day-to-day detailed planning, design, and development of each new community, the *Partnership* would create and appoint a *Local Development Corporation*, as an operating subsidiary, vested with the purposes and appropriate legal powers of its parent non-profit corporation. In cooperation with state and local authorities and communities, representatives of the region would be appointed to an Advisory Board toward good communication on matters affecting the existing communities and governments in the area.

4. Because the relationships between the *Partnership* and the *Local Development Corporations* would be long-lasting, the Corporation team would issue periodic progress reports, budget requests, marketing plans, and audited financial statements on a regular basis. All major land transactions, including grants, would be subject to the approval of the Partnership.

The Congress would invest such powers in the *Partnership* so that its lands and facilities would be deemed federal property and exempt from state and local taxation and development or other regulations. The *Partnership* would be responsible for devising methods for collecting property and other taxes and using and distributing them in a fair and equitable way.

To hasten the marketability of the new MetroCities, the *Partnership* and the *Local Development Corporations* would be permitted to establish incentives by adjusting land and development costs or other potential charges, as well as providing a pollution-free environment, schools, health and recreation facilities, training and employment programs, and cultural programs and facilities. The proposed different funding sources for these dual missions would be as follows:

A. Funds needed to save and upgrade existing metropolitan areas would be allocated by the *Partnership,* utilizing portions of its own funding on a 1:2 basis with periodic Congressional appropriations to the *National Partnership for MetroCities.* The Partnership would put up one third of the funds to be matched by two thirds from the Congress. It would serve as the non-profit conduit for such funding, dealing directly with central cities, suburban and county governments, local and national non-profits, and citizen groups in each of the regions that elected to participate in this bold program.

B. Funds for the new MetroCities, as well as the matching share for existing metropolitan cities, would be raised by issuing long-term revenue bonds pledging the net revenues and available properties of the *National Partnership* but guaranteed by the U.S. Government. Its initial functions, in this regard, would be to determine locations for initial new MetroCities and to purchase or obtain control of sites large enough to accommodate populations up to 500,000 people, at each location, with all the related functions of a green and sustainable modern city.

The *Partnership* would be geared to entering into public and private partnerships and joint development programs, including arrangements with private development companies, homebuilders, commercial and industrial developers and builders, public agencies, non-profit entities, and other relationships that would foster the sound and timely development of the new communities.

Funds for the existing metropolitan cities would be mainly in the form of matching grants that would be Federal investments in the enhancement and rebuilding of those areas. Funds for the new MetroCities, including any required up-front advances for operations, would be a debt of the *Partnership* and subject to repayment from the sale of revenue bonds, raising equity and eventual development revenues. As each new MetroCity moved into a positive financial position, its surplus funds would be utilized for matching grants for existing metropolitan cities and any ongoing expenses of the ensuing new communities. Over the decades of development, after bond-holders were paid off, any surplus funds would be paid into the U.S. Treasury.

Observation
A Legacy from More Caring Times

New York City has about four million dwelling units, from rat-infested basement hovels to $25 million penthouses overlooking Central Park. About five percent, or 200,000, are owned and operated as Public housing serving the poor, the underemployed and the underpaid. As a mainstay of President Roosevelt's New Deal, the Federal Public Housing Administration promoted, funded, and continually subsidized two million homes nationwide. This program allowed the City to demolish the worst of tenements.

Gnawed away at by Republicans and often ignored by Democrats, Public Housing as a resource and haven for low-income families for seventy years, has struggled to survive. Modeled after historic European housing welfare concepts, the very concept has fallen from the public's sense of responsibility, presumably because the majority of tenants happen to be Black! Many moved from the South to escape the cruelty of segregation and to seize the opportunity of working for a living, no matter how marginal.

New York City's Housing Authority, serving 400,000 citizens in 2,600 buildings, is an enormous enterprise in the public interest. Although it has increased rents and reduced maintenance, shrinking Federal support has forced the Authority into the red.

One good solution has been to sell or lease unused parking lots and potential housing sites not likely to be built on by the Authority. Such surplus parcels will be sold subject to their being built for middle-income families. Mixed income neighborhoods have worked well. With private housing prices zooming upward in the City, working folks need a break.

Chapter 8.
Lessons Learned from New Towns

The British New Town program grew directly out of the pre-1945 garden city movement, responsible for the building of Letchworth in 1903 and Welwyn Garden City in 1919. These innovative communities served as models for the first wave of post-war New Towns. The entire experience of 50 years of building thirty-three towns, largely from scratch, has well served the country as forerunners for new and integrated urban areas over the coming decades.

It is important, especially for American readers, to understand the size and scale of England. Not including Ireland or Scotland, the English portion of Great Britain is only about 400 miles north and south and 200 miles wide. It is about one half the size of California with a total population approximating 50 million. In 2007, California, a state with significant mountainous areas has a population of 32 million.

It is also important to note that England has always had a highly centralized government ruled from London and, based on the periodic strength of the Labor Party, had a strong program of government housing for the working classes.

Just after World War II, the Labor Government proposed a New Towns Program to relieve the population and housing pressure on London and promised that these new settlements would be located in the countryside, provide new affordable housing, jobs, schools, and all the amenities of a small town.

Because no local planning agencies were adequate to the job, the sites were declared national property and nationally known professional planning teams were put to work. Cooperation with local governments was required but the central government people made all the decisions.

There was an early bias against bringing in private builders and developers into what were to be essentially public projects. In later years, due to both political and financial considerations, there was a healthy use of private expertise and funding under public agency control. However, each New Town project was actually planned and built by individual public New Town Development Corporations. These were supervised and funded by the central government. The local Corporations were not required to live by the rules and regulations of the existing local governments.

The Development Corporations had powers to acquire, own, manage, and dispose of land and property, undertake building operations and utilities and anything else necessary for the new community. An element in their long-term success was their ability to purchase large tracts of land at rural values and eventually lease or sell improved properties at urban values. Each Corporation also had the freedom to donate land to serve social interests in the town.

They also had aggressive and competitive marketing programs especially when it came to attracting job-creating companies. Although there was healthy competition between the new communities, they also worked together on their common interests.

As the program matured, the new town developers were more inclined to give local people some say in the design and development process. However, the Development Corporations were highly goal-oriented and did not spend much time on local discussions.

The original thrust of the program was to absorb London's "overspill." In the 1990s, it was determined that these projects had accomplished 90% of their projected goals by 1991. Despite criticisms of being too slow to develop, the New Towns were found to be very strong in the fields of land acquisition, the provision of infrastructure, community planning, and house building construction.

Despite periodic objections from the Treasury, new town funding in the form of long-term loans remained consistent throughout its fifty-plus year development period. As national housing subsidy methods changed over the years, some towns were penalized by having to borrow at higher rates.

As private builders played an ever-growing role in housing production, they continued to object to the Development Corporation's controls over design and pricing. They did not object to discounts on land for their projects.

The New Towns were also considered quite successful in three areas: the provision of good quality affordable (mostly rental) housing, the provision of "social capital" for schools, health and community facilities, and the creation of socially mixed and balanced communities.

The entire New Towns program suffered financial setbacks in the 1980s so that suspension of interest and debt write-offs gave them a black mark from a financial point of view. The proponents of the program had no way of knowing when or if a recession would occur any more than the U.S. Government could predict the several that have occurred over the last forty years. The Savings and Loan debacle and the Chrysler and Lockheed bailouts come to mind.

The New Town planners initially projected that a town of 50,000 could be built in ten years. That would call for 20,000 dwelling units or 2,000 per year every year for ten years. That goal would have been reachable because they were mainly building rental units and only later were houses offered for sate.

Although it was assumed and stated that the New Towns would show a profit, there was little evidence that there was a sense of urgency on that issue. Different conditions in levels of market acceptance, the creation of suitable jobs, and a myriad of political and financing problems would have easily affected the pace of development.

In 1993, it was calculated that 57% of the investment had been returned and later accounting showed that, as a whole, the program had returned 100% of the investment. During that fifty-year period, there had been some write-offs of interest due so that it is difficult to know exactly what the larger financial picture was.

The British New Towns program was meant to meet human needs for decent housing, schools, health clinics, ball and cricket fields, hiking trails, and many other public works. It was not viewed as a real estate transaction. Their national public policies were to prevent London from being overdeveloped and used housing and urban development programs to make the great diversion take place. One of the great motivations of the planners and builders of the New Towns was to improve the quality of design of the massive housing developments. They looked down on what private developers had done and saw the public effort as a chance to upgrade both aesthetics and livability.

In the field of land acquisition, the earliest managers purchased only enough land for the first phases of the New Town. When they had to go back to continue to purchase property for future phases, their naivety resulted in higher prices. As a result, acquisition policies were changed so that the Corporations would buy enough land for the entire community and its permanent open space. That approach further fortified the likelihood that, if the carrying charges were relatively low, future dispositions would produce a profit.

The thirty-three towns were essentially financed by long-term loans (sixty years) at a fixed rate of interest, starting at 3%. Those rates were later raised, which had a negative effect on the performance of the second- and third-phase towns. The financing of rental housing was a separate operation, and the Towns were treated like other municipalities. They received initial construction funding and then annual support money for maintenance and operations. That formula was used by the Public Housing Administration in the U.S. for several decades.

By the 1970s, there was a major decision to sell land to private developers and let them provide their own financing. Previously, land had been sold to businesses and industries that created jobs for the new residents. Land and related improvements had also been given for public and private institutions that worked to improve the quality of life in the new communities.

Much of the physical planning for the New Towns was done in an era when automobile reliance and ownership was quite low. People in small towns were used to walking and especially bicycling. Though the weather in central England is often damp and dreary, snow is never very heavy, so biking around was not much of a problem. Bus service to factories was provided, and train service to larger cities was excellent. The growth of auto ownership since the 1970s has put a strain on the road systems and the relatively small car parks. Also, after World War II, women generally returned to homemaking and child rearing until recent decades. In recent years, child-care centers have become more critical and the Development Corporations have played an important role in providing them.

On the subject of governance, the Development Corporations saw themselves as enlightened public servants who ran practically everything including being the master landlord for large numbers of housing. However, responsibilities were divided in that education and health facilities and services were provided directly by the national Ministries.

As the towns grew, various elections were held to fill local government seats, and some tension arose between them and the Corporations. This is similar to that which occurs in large-scale community projects in the United States.

In the late 1950s, as several of the New Towns started showing a profit and built up assets, the Conservative Government acted to prevent those assets from getting in the hands of the predominantly Labor controlled local district authorities and so created the Commission on New Towns. That new government agency was granted planning responsibilities, ownership of rental housing, and commercial and industrial land assets. Over the ensuing decades, the Commission's powers were changed and it has ended up primarily as a development and disposal vehicle.

In managing its open spaces around the new towns, many were lauded for the protection of wildlife and natural habitats. Some were criticized for non-urban planning and having their communities too spread out and inconvenient.

The Special Case of Milton Keynes

In the 1960s, after nearly twenty new towns with planned populations from 50,000 to 75,000 were underway, it was recognized that the program was too limited to help absorb the growing populations of several major cities. A new city of 250,000 was planned and located forty-five miles north of London, half way between London and Birmingham. An area already containing many villages was chosen and eventually included 21,760 acres with an existing population of about 40,000.

In designing the proposed new city, the planners broke away from the conventional concentric circle concept and, with the aid of Professor Melvin Webber of the University of California at Berkeley, adopted a gridiron pattern laid out in one-kilometer squares. This concept allowed the city to grow in a linear fashion recognizing that the development period would be longer than experienced in the smaller towns. This plan resulted in 100, one-kilometer squares that served as the basis for neighborhood planning.

By 2001, its population had reached 207,000. The new city has a 65,000 seat Concert bowl, a 1,400 seat theatre, a full range of educational, social, and cultural facilities as well as professional football, ice hockey, and basketball teams. Its cyclists and hikers enjoy 200 miles of paths in the green areas.

Although the community has a healthy employment base, commuting is popular. In 2002, plans for a major regional business, shopping, residential mixed-use center were announced and is being developed. The population goal has been expanded to 300,000. This remarkable development program accomplished by a less than prosperous country, half the size of California, serves as a good marker for thinking about the future of American cities.

American New Towns

The best current source on the subject of American New Towns is *Reforming Suburbia* (2005) by Ann Forsyth, now a professor and Chair of Urban Design and Director of the Design Center for American Urban Landscape at the University of Minnesota in the Twin Cities, MN. This book is a scholarly and analytical examination of the three foremost new towns: Columbia, MD; Irvine Ranch, CA; and The Woodlands, TX.

Two of the massive projects were headed by entrepreneurial businessmen determined to prove that the urban scene could be built in a better way and the third was originally directed by high-powered professionals under the guidance of a family that had inherited a huge California ranch, put together in 1895.

James Rouse, Founder of The Rouse Company and Columbia, was a wise, thoughtful, and caring man who had succeeded in the mortgage banking and shopping center worlds but yearned to make a difference by showing the way in new city development. His view was that American cities and suburbs looked and functioned as they did because no one had grasped the opportunity and potential benefits of pulling all the pieces of community development into one cohesive, synergistic whole.

The conceptual leaders in planning and developing the urban portions of the 93,000 acre Irvine Ranch were the famed architect-planner William Pereira and, later, Irvine Presidents Bill Mason and Ray Watson. The latter two led the extensive development and marketing from 1966 to 1977. Their efforts were hampered by conflicts with family heirs and formation or expansion of municipalities covering parts of the urbanizing ranch.

George Mitchell, owner of a large oil and gas company, was also disturbed by disorganized suburban development and the conditions in the inner cities. He saw the key challenge in new town building was in respecting and saving of habitats for nature and open spaces for humans. His original land holdings were about 17,000 acres, later expanded to 27,000. He was greatly influenced by Professor and Landscape Architect Ian McHarg of the University of Pennsylvania. The new community was named The Woodlands and much of its professional leadership people were alumni of the Rouse Company and Columbia, including Richard Browne who spent twenty years guiding the development. The Woodlands was the only one of the three that applied for and received a HUD guarantee under Title X of the Housing and Urban Development Act of 1968.

That Federal Guarantee program approved and issued guarantees of loans for acquisition and infrastructure for fifteen communities ranging from the 336 acres for the New-Town-in-Town, Cedar-Riverside in Minneapolis to the then 17,000 acre Woodlands. The total area of the proposed towns was over 800,000 acres with a combined target population of 750,000 or an average of 50,000 residents per town. Many of the new town sponsors were business neophytes and several of the proposed locations were far from major markets. Almost all were undercapitalized and were approved as a result of political pressure.

By 1983, all but one of the Federally-supported new communities went bankrupt or failed to meet debt service requirements. Only The Woodlands, essentially financed by the Mitchell Oil and Gas Company, survived the Federal New Town experience. President Nixon had effectively cancelled all Federal guarantees that raised havoc with the HUD officials trying to assist the New Towns. In 1994, the Federal Government was forced to take punitive action against the surviving developers.

Columbia luckily had no opportunity to participate in the Federal program because it was launched in 1963. After secretly purchasing over 2,000 acres in Howard County, MD, the county directly between Washington and Baltimore, and finding a general willingness for farmers to sell at a reasonable price, Rouse approached the head of the Connecticut General Life Insurance Company (CG) in Hartford, CT. Frazier Wilde, who has risen from office boy to Chief Executive of CG, listened to Rouse's concept of a complete new town that would not only be a landmark in rational community development, would make a good profit over time, and would serve as a model for other developers in the future.

The financial plan called for the acquisition of 12,000 acres for a town of 100,000 people at a projected land cost of about $20 million. Rouse would pay up to $1 million for planning, legal, and other pre-development expenses if CG would put up $24 million for land acquisition. Rouse proclaimed that the worst thing that could happen is that CG would make a lot of money over time. Wilde agreed and the purchase program went ahead, in deep secrecy, with the buying of 144 farms for $24 million in cash. The 14,000 acres assembled represented about 10% of the County.

Once the land acquisition financing was in place, Rouse authorized William Finley, previously recruited from the National Capital Planning Commission (NCPC) in Washington, DC, to bring on a planning team. He brought in Mort Hoppenfeld as Chief Planner and Bob Tennenbaum as Architect-Planner, both from the NCPC. This trio was responsible for the planning and design of Columbia with the daily participation of James Rouse, the visionary who guided the process.

After a year of intensive social, economic, and physical planning, the Columbia Plan was presented to the highly conservative County Government. (See The Columbia Planning Process) After a powerful marketing campaign, the General Plan and total flexible zoning was approved. The Plan called for 33,000 dwelling units, 25% of the land to be dedicated to open space and community facilities and 25% for business and industry to assure the essential economic balance between residential development and tax paying, non-residential properties.

With the Plan approved, Rouse raised another $26 million from another insurance company and David Rockefeller's Chase Manhattan Bank. From early 1965 to the summer of 1967, the site was a frenzy of earthmoving, the building of dams, roads offices, homes, apartments, recreation facilities, a music pavilion, and other amenities. In June, 1967, Columbia, "The Next America," was opened to the public. Over twenty-nine years, through recessions, storms, and financial troubles, the New Town was completed with 34,000 dwelling units, over 80,000 jobs, a balanced tax base, twenty-seven schools and 30% of the land in permanent open space. Although each of these huge projects had different financing components, different political issues, and varied emphases, there were a great many similar problems and methods for solving them. An overview focuses on these points:

1. There is no doubt that building a large community that takes several decades to complete is fraught with risks. They revolve around land acquisition and control, the long-term commitment

of financial partners, and how local politics evolve based on new residents and changing politicians.

In the "get-rich-quick" mentality of the 21st Century, it seems unlikely that any financial institution would put up millions of dollars for a twenty to twenty-five year project without some reliable guarantee other than a mortgage on the land. The term "patient money" is now an oxymoron.

2. Private land assembly is extremely difficult. Rouse and his associates bought land through a series of "straw" entities in a nine-month assembly period. If any leaks had occurred, the entire financial structure that served as the basis for the planned new town could have been ruined. Large out-parcels can create competitive havoc with new community planning or create dangerous competitors eager to share in the benefits of the massive development.

3. It is important that new town developers state their community development goals early so that the general information can evoke as much positive response as possible. Potential competitors or enemies can be disarmed if the goals stated assuage fears and muster allies from those who will benefit from the project. In Columbia, residents of existing half-acre lot subdivisions eventually favored the new town development for fear that the alternative was dozens more of subdivisions like their own on well water and septic tanks.

4. It is critical to be very realistic about the time it will take to obtain approvals, permits and, as necessary, any public agency construction essential to the project. Since time is money, any opponents will know that if they can drag out the process, it will hurt the project. If the developer expresses any urgency over time, it will assuredly come back to bite him.

5. Among the many entities that need to be kept informed of the new community's plans are nearby cities, counties, and special districts that could be affected by a massive new development. Depending on the size and scope of the project, other jurisdictions may see it as competitive for cultural facilities, road funding, or other important aspects.

6. The recruitment of institutional allies early in the planning, such as a university, a high-tech company, or a sports team could be useful in building support for the new project. In Columbia, bringing in the health planning team from the famous Johns Hopkins Hospital added credibility to the planning effort.

7. There is likely to be a dilemma in seeking public agency approval for the entire community that will likely take several decades to complete. Depending on whether the controlling government agency has mechanisms in place to deal with large-scale projects, it may be difficult to avoid having to determine housing types and densities by location that won't be developable for many years. A better solution would be to obtain a holistic legal entitlement of land uses by units or acres that would allow flexibility in the future.

8. The only thing that is absolutely known about the future is that unexpected events will occur that will affect a long-range development project. Radical downturn in the residential market, high levels of inflation, utility system breakdowns, investors' financial troubles or other disasters will assuredly happen. The financial model for the new community should contain safeguards, such as a rolling reserve for carrying charges or cost overruns beyond the control of the developer. Columbia suffered through two recessions, the developer's internal financial problems, and a major County utility system breakdown.

9. The first way the public will view and value the new community is how the residential areas look and feel. A major and critical component of any new town development program is the plan and method of installing residential infrastructure, utilizing home builders, financing land sales, careful multi-family development, and the all-important control of quality. Homebuilders are confident they know what the public wants or they wouldn't stay in business. The community developer may have a different vision. This will be a continuing conflict throughout the development period. Price, pace, and appearance will be the key concerns.

10. It is easy for the new town planners to propose setting aside large natural and environmentally sensitive areas as permanent open space. As important is the question of who will design, build,

and maintain the open spaces so they can be used and enjoyed by the residents. These responsibilities can be very expensive and controversial.

Relying on a public agency to maintain and manage the woods, plantings, paths, bridges, signs, shelters, and other improvements is chancy unless it is bound by an unbreakable contract. A version of a homeowners' association is an obvious alternative but tricky because changing board members can radically alter the budgets and management competence. Reviewing public agencies will be very interested in the solution to this knotty problem.

11. Another absolutely critical responsibility, again depending on the size and scope of the new community, will be assuring an adequate future tax base to protect the homeowners and apartment owners from onerous tax or fee increases to pay for the variety of facilities and services proposed and promised by the overall developer.

Attracting property-tax paying businesses and industries is the long-term key to the success of the community. And, of course, to whom they pay their "taxes" is really vital. If those payments go to the local government, then the new community residents may not control the use of funds collected. The Columbia experience of creating a town-wide private "taxing" district is a huge success. Forsyth's book offers a complete description of the process.

Actually attracting and recruiting the tax- or fee-paying, non-residential, job-creating companies is even more important than The Columbia planning process is being described because the land acquisition, financing, and broad-based planning undertaken by The Rouse Company was so broad in scope and in depth that it could likely serve as a preliminary model for future new MetroCities.

Rouse approached the building of a complete new town or city in a totally holistic way. His primary notion was that the man-made environment should be designed and constructed as a way of serving the growth and full development of people. Everything else was important but secondary.

People meant everyone who might choose to live, work, teach, pray, sell, buy, suffer, or die there. He believed that humans respond to positive, caring, and meaningful treatment and that much of how people carry out their chosen activities is hindered or helped by the organization and condition of their environment.

That, in turn, meant the homes, the streets, the walks and paths, the views, the greenery, the schools, the shops, the work places, and the managers and governments that provided and governed them. This somewhat Utopian view of life was directly expressed by Rouse in his famous talk in 1963 at the University of California at Berkeley, titled "It Can Happen Here."

Just as we do today, he started to talk about growth. He said, "Coming growth will be so enormous that it will transform the face and form of our cities and our country for the next twenty years." He pointed out that the problem of planning was that no one was asking the right questions.

He continued, "If we were really trying to create inspired, concerned, and loving people, might not this begin to influence the kind of plans we would unfold; and might it not point the way to answers we are not now perceiving?"

This was the question he asked all the planners and advisors, from those involved in walking the land, road engineers, health care professionals, educators, economists, psychologists, and all who were invited to participate in the overall planning of his new community.

He said boldly, "With the resources that already exist among us, who will generate a new, creative thrust that will not only produce new communities but will release among the people in them the potential for the noblest civilizations the world has ever known?"

With the audience not knowing about his specific goals, he concluded, "The building of this civilization still needs to be done and that the lofty goal not achieved yesterday might still be reached tomorrow!" This 1963 talk became the watchword for the work that followed in planning Columbia.

Rouse's ideals are as legitimate in the 21st century as they were in 1963. The only question is whether the Nation's resources, human, financial, and technical, will be mustered to even ask the right questions on behalf of its burgeoning population.

Even before the era of environmental sensitivity and the rules and regulations that followed, the first consultant hired by the planning team was Dr. Paul Sears, a Yale ecologist, to guide the analysis of the land and its inhabitants. This study became one basis for structuring the 3,500 acres proposed for open space and community facilities in and around the 10,000 acres programmed for residential and business/industrial uses.

Rouse's love of small towns fit perfectly into the hierarchy of community design within which nine villages of 10,000 to 15,000 people would be defined by open spaces, parkways and other natural barriers. Although no conclusions had been yet reached about the direction and methodology of the future model public school system, it eventually became both the backbone and the community structure around which all other factors would revolve.

The planning process was early divided into physical, social, and economic studies and analyses. The first included understanding the nuances of the rolling and partially wooded Maryland countryside. The effect of gravity on utility systems weighed heavily on preliminary site planning. Consultant Alan Voorhees, a DC transportation planner was bought in to discuss road and highway alternates. The goal was to balance the aesthetic aspects of community development with the realistic demands of auto travel and service.

Rouse brought in Nelson Foote, a sociologist with GE whom he had met in consulting with the Rockefeller holdings in upper New York State. Foote's keen observations about the American psyche and trends brought deep understanding to all parties in the planning process.

Finley recruited Bob Gladstone, an urban and housing economist, to advise on housing and business markets, population analyses, and the employment trends in the Baltimore-Washington corridor, already in a growth mode. Gladstone also was instrumental in structuring the initial financial model for the entire community.

To give each consultant the benefit of the other's experience and thinking, a "Work Group" consisting of fourteen experts was assembled for both broad explorations of the urban scene as well as revelations of what the cutting edges were in each of their fields. In addition to Foote, Voorhees, and Gladstone, Dr. Paul Lemkau, a health care systems physician from the JohnHopkins in Baltimore, provided overview for a community-wide health-care system. The Kaiser Permanente Plan in California was studied and admired. To chair the sessions, Dr. Don Michael, a Harvard Social Psychologist, was recruited. Among his requirements were that Rouse, Finley, and Hoppenfeld had to faithfully attend all meetings of the group.

Finley hired Henry Bain, a Washington advisor on local government, to create a "psychogram" or a diagram of the functional arrangements and relationships between all the apparent leaders in Howard County, the site of the new town. His deep insight into the politics of the rural county proved invaluable when a disclosure strategy was prepared for sharing the ultimate intentions of the land purchaser-developer.

Other contributors to the wealth of knowledge available to help the planners included Wayne Thompson, City Manager of Oakland, CA, and an early mentor of Finley's. Professor Chet Rapkin, a housing guru from Penn, Harvard Educator Christopher Jencks and Robert Crawford, a recreation administrator in Philadelphia, brought wisdom and some warnings to the gatherings.

After several sessions, the consensus was that four broad goals should be established for the new community:

1. To respect the land
2. To create a place to encourage human growth

3. To create a whole city, not just a residential suburb
4. To make a profit

The experts naturally kept suggesting possible barriers and negative conditions that would likely prevent reaching many positive outcomes. Rouse's response to those "caveats" was that they were there to provide positive insights and leave the worrying to the project's developer and planners.

In several cases, such as health care, education, and alternate methods of governance, papers were prepared and then dissected by the other members. Dr. Herb Gans, an urban sociologist studying Levittown in Long Island, brought a down-to-earth view of life in suburbia. Rouse offered, "We don't expect to plan the perfect community, simply the best we can envision!" No single system or ideas discussed at the group sessions ended up as being dominant. However, Rouse and the planners had plenty of advice to think about.

By chance, there was only one woman in the Work Group. Antonia Chayes was a Washington lawyer and who had served on the President's Commission on the Status of Women. The gist of the conversations about women in American society was that they were pushing hard and gaining ground in many areas of the economy and society.

The subject of race was another story. Columbia would be built in Southern Maryland, a border state with strongholds of white supremacy. Rouse maintained that there was no way anyone would try to build a segregated city in the 1960s, even if it were possible. It was clear that by that time the schools were integrated and so would be all neighborhoods. He rejected any talk of quotas or special recruiting. His position, for all to hear, was that this new town would be open to all who chose to live or work or teach there.

It should be noted that, even though it is only thirty minutes to Baltimore, a heavily Black city, Columbia's Black population has hovered at about 17% for over twenty-five years. And this ratio has stayed about the same in the face of remarkable increases in home prices, beyond anyone's control. The concept of racial neutrality was stated everywhere it was appropriate and it became a well-known fact in the then minority areas of Baltimore and Washington.

The Work group met every two weeks for about four months. Although records of the conversations were taped, they were never transcribed nor was a final report issued. As the physical planners proceeded, they assimilated the various institutional concepts that the Group has discussed. Various staff members were assigned the tasks of following up to make some of those institutions come to life. They became real in the fields of community-wide health care, a radical, highly-rated public school system, a community-owned parks and recreation system open to the public, and an ecumenical system of religious facilities in the place of conventional churches.

A 3,500-seat covered, plus lawn seating, music pavilion, similar to Tanglewood, was designed by Frank Gehry and Dave O'Malley and became the summer home of the Washington National Symphony. Many other victories in the cultural and educational world came into being through the creative dedication of the Rouse Company staff.

During the two-year initial construction period, over 100 sub-projects were underway. Prior to its opening in June 1967, road and utility systems, model homes and apartments, dams, lakes, recreation facilities, office buildings, industrial centers, shops, a supermarket, plazas and fountains, a golf course and club, tennis center, pools, a path system, convenience centers, and pre-schools were designed and built. In addition to the pre-computer financial model that became the tool for fiscal control, another PERT system for development coordination was put into place to keep order in the chaos.

On opening night, Vice President Humphrey was there and Van Cliburn played, accompanied by the National Symphony.

The original Columbia Plan laid out nine villages consisting of twenty-seven neighborhoods each with an elementary-school, a pre-school center and playground, a park and pool, and a convenience store all to be walked to via paved paths and underpasses under busy streets. Every neighborhood had apartments, townhouses, and single-family units in a wide range of prices.

Eventually, twenty-seven schools were built in Columbia by the Howard County School Board. The developer donated finished sites to the Board at the locations called for in the Plan.

The "Downtown" was to consist of a multi-department store enclosed mall with adjacent office towers, restaurants, a main library and, hopefully, a "Tivoli Gardens" similar to that ancient amusement-cultural-fun complex in Copenhagen, Denmark. That element of the Plan never came to fruition, but the Downtown lakefront is the primary event site for the new town.

Special sites were reserved and given to an ecumenical housing group dedicated to building affordable housing. A ten percent minimum of all housing quotas was adopted for supported housing that was more-or-less followed in later years.

As the first town-wide development plan was finally pulled together, a test against the financial model pronounced it infeasible. The open space greenbelt around the town ate up too much land, especially in the light of the fact that the major stream valleys ran diagonally through the 14,000 acres.

Densities were increased, some niceties were cut back, and the plan was modified to meet the promised profit margins, in line with the long-term schedule, as promised to the financial institutions that by then had $50 million invested.

Columbia, the new town completed in the 1990s, is a joy to visit and tour. There are no overhead wires, no billboards, no strip centers, no garish signs. But there are millions of street trees, miles of safe pathways, clubs, and social groups to meet every human need, a community foundation, occasionally troubling teenagers, colleges, wonderfully named streets and places and, true to the early promises, over 60,000 jobs.

The two areas of disappointment are the all but abandoned community-wide bus system and the runaway prices for homes and apartments. An automated transit system was planned and the right-of-way for it was originally reserved. The Federal rapid transit funding program did try to fund it but was beat out by a student-serving system at West Virginia University in Morgantown, West Virginia.

On the subject of housing prices, there was an opportunity to put price controls on certain re-sales but Rouse disagreed with that approach. He opined that the market would produce sufficient low-end housing and that gentrification would not occur. That was one area in which he was wrong.

A more detailed coverage of the planning and development process can be found in *Better Places, Better Lives,* an excellent biography of James W. Rouse by Joshua Olsen (2003).

As touched on earlier, the tentative and arbitrary allocation of land, 50% for residential uses, 25% for open space, and 25% for economic development went into the financial models for testing. In general, the distribution worked although open space jumped to 30% in later iterations of the development plan.

During the planning process, over 500 meetings were held with residents of the twenty large and small existing subdivisions in the area to discover their fears and concerns and to offer and guarantee physical solutions to satisfy them. That process eventually resulted in absolutely no public opposition to the plan for new town of 100,000 people to be built in their midst.

Observation
Britain Leaps Ahead with Zero-Carbon "Eco-Towns"

UK Housing Minister announced in March, 2007, that the government would welcome proposals from local governments and new town corporations for the building of carbon-free towns on Brownfields. Those are sites that could have had some level of contamination or simply have been bypassed in the normal path of housing development.

They envision small towns of 5,000 to 10,000 homes in projects that could lead the way in utilizing technology that could be transferred to older housing in the future. Forty-five local groups have expressed a strong interest in the program. How the Country will eliminate carbon belching trucks and buses is not known. However, the U.S. may learn from the British again.

Observation
A New Term for a New Breakthrough

Two substantial new communities with up to 350,000 and 400,000 population goals are the new crucibles for a powerful mixture of abbreviations that produce a code that will be very important in the language of sustainable cities.

The new term is: cRRescendo (maybe pronounced "see-resendo'9, which stands for: Combined Rational and Renewable Energy Strategies in Cities for Existing and New Dwellings to ensure Optimal quality of life! Quite a mouthful! As acronyms go, it is a difficult job. However, the task is formidable too!

The aim is to integrate a majority of sustainability factors to reduce the use of costly and damaging energy by using the newest technology on a grand scale. These communities will be the important pioneers in the climate-salvation revolution. There is universal acceptance of the idea that consumers will flock to the newer, safer, and cheaper environments.

Almere, the Netherlands, is a new town east of Amsterdam currently housing 175,000 residents with a goal of 350,000 by 2030. Their Environmental Plan commits to an aggressive reduction of C02, RES (Renewable Energy supply) via biomass and solar produced heat, and RUE (Energy efficiency in buildings), education of consumers, and other advanced concepts.

Milton Keynes, Britain's largest new town, now at 215,000, will serve 3,800 people in 1,800 homes with a similar variety of energy management systems using both biomass and gas-fired plants. It is exciting to see what small countries can do while waiting for what the U.S. can do.

Chapter 9.
The Science of Locating New MetroCities

The main purpose in building new MetroCities is to help divert seemingly inevitable urban growth away from the existing metropolitan areas that choose to limit their physical expansion. The diversion is not likely to be identifiable, meaning Chicago would not actually be redirecting the next half million urban-minded people who ordinarily have no choice other than to settle on the outskirts of that great city.

However, if a new MetroCity in central Illinois were an attractive alternative with positive magnetism and powerful financial incentives, a good number of people could make that choice.

The second motive for the new MetroCities is to give families, individuals, and business or institutions the opportunity to locate in a less stressful, healthy, and beautiful new community. The new MetroCities may not appeal to those who choose and can afford to zip into midtown Manhattan for dinner and a show a couple of times a week. They are willing to trade the congestion, the noise, the homeless, and crime for the fun of the big city, and that's part of the charm of America.

New MetroCities will be designed and built with children in mind and opportunities for a ten-minute commute on the light rail compared to the urban rat race so many American wage-earners settle for. If the new MetroCities live up to their promises, as most of Columbia, MD, has, they will be happy places with unlimited choices for all.

Teams of planners, engineers, biologists, and other scientists will examine whole undeveloped regions for potential sites. Their analyses will include a close look at terrain, natural features, soil conditions, water supplies, road access, air traffic, climate, and environmentally-sensitive conditions such as Brownfields.

They will also record Native American lands, military installations, rail lines and connections, ownership patterns, legal or other barriers to development, state and local attitudes, sources of employees, and availability of construction materials. Federal law requires that any planned major project prepare an Environmental Impact Study spelling out the potential impact such development may have on natural resources, animal and bird habitats, and roads and other systems. Such a study would be done on several potential sites and evaluated before recommendations are forwarded to policy decision makers. Public hearings would be held at several locations so that all interested parties could voice their reactions to the study and the location.

Potential acquisition prices would guided by the use of independent appraisals. Under the law establishing the *Partnership*, the right of eminent domain for Federal purposes would be granted to it. As is true in most public-purpose purchases, the vast majority of property is obtained through negotiation, and condemnation is used only in extreme cases.

In suggesting potential sites, it should be noted that these possible sites are very preliminary and would require extensive study and investigation after the *Partnership* was created and operational.

1. The New York to Washington, DC, corridor, according to the Census Bureau, is expected to grow from 27.8 to 36.3 million, a gain of 8.5 million. To make a dent in diverting much of that potential growth would require the concerted action of New York, New Jersey, Pennsylvania, Maryland, Virginia, and the District of Columbia, not to mention the hundreds of cities in that corridor.

However, it is such an historically popular super-region, it might be valuable to locate a new MetroCity in central Pennsylvania for those who would like to live within two hours of that crowded coastline but enjoy the benefits of living in a new kind of environment.

2. Although projected growth in the arc created by Detroit, MI, Cleveland and Columbus, OH, and Indianapolis to the west is limited, if they chose to slow their sprawl, a new MetroCity in the vicinity of Lima, OH, could be a location.

3. Similarly, the Chicago Metropolitan area is projected to grow from its present population of 9.4 to 9.9 million. An overflow location could be in central Illinois.

4. Florida, with a population of 18 million is projected to house 32 million by 2030. With Miami, Orlando, Tampa, and Jacksonville all growing, a prospective site for southbound sun-seeking folks could be at a new MetroCity in southwestern Georgia.

5. The Houston-Dallas corridor is also growing fast enough for Texas to rival Florida in terms of new growth. A potential site might be near Abilene well north of Austin.

6. Arizona and New Mexico, the leading Sunbelt states, could stand a well-planned MetroCity instead of the thousands of acres of single family cottages strewn over the landscape. A site in the south-central portion of New Mexico could work if the physical conditions are not too difficult.

7. Los Angeles is the grand theatre of sprawl with a capital S. Its famous smog, freeway gridlock, and endless commutes make it a candidate for diversion. If the thousands of problems could be solved, a site near Needles, CA, close to the Arizona line might work, Summer temperatures there are fierce but a low mountain valley might be found.

8. The San Francisco Bay Area is now over 5 million. With the ocean and the bay, bridges and mountains, they are running out of room. Some people are commuting two hours from the Central Valley. To divert some of the coming growth, a MetroCity site near Tonopah, NV, might attract settlers from the East and Far East.

It should be further understood that this listing of possible sites is purely speculative without the analysis of detailed topographic or climatological maps. This entire process is an exercise in spatial planning, a new term in America.

European Spatial Planning is a book by Andreas Falidu, a planner and scholar who works to understand and speculate on the issues of urbanization and its effects on adjacent countries in the European Union. He was an eminent scholar at the University of California at Berkeley and Harvard and is now Professor of Spatial Policy Systems at the University of Nijmegen in the Netherlands. In 2000, he came to the U.S. to meet with planners and thinkers at the Lincoln Institute of Land Policy in Cambridge, MA. A Senior Fellow there, Armando Carbonell and Robert D. Yaro of the New York Regional Plan Association led the discussions including the fact that no one in America is focusing on the enormous expansion of urbanization here and the runaway sprawl with its insidious side effects.

Yaro wrote the epilogue for American city and regional planners. He asked the question, "Imagine what the impact would be were the Federal government to provide financial incentives for states and metropolitan regions to collaborate across borders...to integrate transportation, economic development, and environmental strategies?" It would have an enormous, positive impact on the quality of urban life in America. It would be expected that a state and its local governments might be fearful and suspicious of a Federal program to build huge urban projects in or around their backyard. However, when it is understood that a new MetroCity with 225,000 dwelling units and millions to be spent to bring business and industry could be a financial windfall to their treasuries, attitudes could turn positive. Each MetroCity™ would trigger massive expenditures and thousands of jobs over a generation.

A completed 500,000 population MetroCity would represent a combined public and private expenditure of $40 to $50 Billion. Just the housing alone would create over 20,000 construction jobs on a *steady* basis. Business and industrial buildings and improvements would call for 120 million square feet of construction or over four million square feet per year. That is the equivalent of three, five department-store enclosed mall centers every year. Infrastructure costs would also be in the $billions.

Local officials would be concerned about their powers to approve or disapprove specific projects. They might also be worried about too many new voters. There is no question that a new MetroCity plopped down in a rural area would make big waves. It would change the lives of local people forever. It would also bring a new kind of prosperity.

When New York Governor Nelson Rockefeller proposed, and the State legislature concurred, to create the New York State Urban Development Corporation, its task was to create 30,000 new middle-income housing units throughout the State, including in New York City. The Corporation had the powers of Eminent Domain but rarely used them. It could override local zoning and other building restrictions. It did that and produced some of the finest housing in the State.

The *National Partnership for MetroCities* and its Local Development Corporations will have the obligation to treat state and local officials and residents with the utmost respect and dignity. Service on the Local Development Corporation should be a privilege and an honor, hopefully attracting the best of the local citizens. Because the *Partnership* is a non-profit corporation in the public interest, its business must be transparent and consistent with good business practices.

Observation
A Grand Addition to a Super-Park

A combination of business and non-profit operators have put together a deal to increase preservation in the largest publicly protected park in the U.S. Created in 1892, its six million acres is half public and half private, the latter being used as timberlands, camps, private farms, and scattered homes. The Nature Conservancy led the $110,000,000 acquisition from private owners to add 161,000 acres to the Adirondack Park.

The plan is to continue proper timbering, renew private leases, and keep large areas wild forever in order to maintain the biological diversity and ecological protection. Private funding to cover the purchase price will be sought by the Conservancy. The purchase price came to $686 per acre. The new owners will continue to pay property taxes to the thirty-one towns in six counties in which the property is located.

The Nature Conservancy has raised hundreds of millions of dollars to protect crucial property over the last thirty years during which the federal acquisition of national park lands has dwindled.

Observation
Can the Sunbelt Get Too Hot?

There are two kinds of people in Arizona. Some go north for the summer, the others stay and talk about the heat. One of the differences between Arizona and Florida is that the western heat is "dry" and the southeastern climate is "humid." The other difference is that Florida has 2,400 miles of beaches and a practically guaranteed breeze.

However, Arizona, particularly Phoenix and Tucson, is growing like crazy with people from the middle-west and colder climes along the Canadian border. No question, in the winter, it is a golfers' paradise and a golf cart driver's delight.

However, stretching out thousands of single family homes, wide asphalt streets, huge parking lots for commercial centers and office buildings and thirsty golf courses and lawns do not lead to the right answer to the heat-getting-worse syndrome. Planting palm trees instead of shade trees does not seem like an idea whose time has come. Sloped red-tiled roofs become radiators that absorb the sun's heat.

Those who stay to complain may not worry about the cost of air conditioning or the future water supply, but someone should. Apparently, the combined heat radiated from structures and the growing concern about global warming has not yet hit the mentalities of those eager buyers or those public officials who are supposed to think about such things. When the temperature there exceeds 120 degrees, maybe someone will start asking questions rather than just complaining.

Chapter 10.
A Fork in the Road:

Recommended National Policies on Urban Growth

At this most important intersection along the road of community and national urban development, the nation has several choices. In simplest terms, it can continue with the unfettered growth of metropolitan areas with the resulting consequences of congestion, endless sprawl, the breakdown of systems not designed for such populations, and the further degradation of the environment. Currently, American cities slated for more growth are on a slippery slope toward urban conditions that no one wants but that no one knows how to avoid.

Or it can, with visionary and courageous leadership at national, state, and regional levels, take bold steps to create a political machinery to deal with the crises in center cities, ever more costly suburbs, and the ruination of the countryside. By recognizing the threats inherent in the coming wave of population expansion and the likelihood of where those tens of millions will settle, it should be clearly evident which road to take.

No one pretends that elected and appointed leaders are prone to vision or political courage but, from time to time, the right issues and the right circumstances may present the opportunity to make the right choices. Of course, doing nothing is also a choice. The concepts for metropolitan change presented here are not mysterious or rocket science. They are straight-forward, achievable goals and mechanisms. The enormous accomplishments in Portland, OR, can be tested and touched and be experienced at the cost of a plane ticket. That success story is not applicable to all metropolitan cities but their way of thinking can be molded to fit other sizes and configurations.

Although it is too early to congratulate ourselves, it would seem that our nation is on the road to understanding, accepting, and beginning to tackle the realities of man-made climate change with its threatening global warming. Even in an age of terrorist threats, politicians of almost all stripes are focusing on the critical issues of oil's damage and dependency and the urgent need for other forms of useable energy. Few would have predicted, a decade ago, this sea change of scientific understanding at the citizens' level.

We need not stretch our imagination too much to know we can come to grips with the issues of overpopulation, how to help old cities not designed for such demands, and the enormous human and financial costs of the growth track we are on. On the whole, those who have decried the negatives of urban sprawl have offered no alternate solutions to the problems caused by the thirst for new housing, new infrastructure, and other community-serving improvements. The recommendations in this book will be difficult but not impossible to achieve. Fortunately, our nation has the know-how to deal with the hardware issues of controlling urban expansion and the building of new metropolitan cities.

But there are no medicines on the shelf to deal with the deep, complex problems of inner city residents plagued by low skills, too many children, weakened family structure, and cultural deficiencies. The crushing anguish of poverty has no easy solutions. To date, minimal safety net programs have been hampered by overlapping or gaps in assignments, uneven funding, and no real commitment to lift the least fortunate out of their misery.

As David Brooks reported in the *New York Times* in July, 2007, "You have to holistically change the environment that structures behavior." He pointed out that the only presidential candidates who have even addressed the issues of urban poverty were Edwards and Obama and that even they prescribed different approaches toward long-term solutions. It should be obvious that urban poverty is everybody's problem. It will not go away; it will only get worse. It will never be obliterated unless regional, state, and national leaders accept the need for searching out solutions as their challenge.

Many national foundations, including Ford and Enterprise, have launched massive efforts to upgrade housing conditions for the poor in dozens of cities. The Enterprise Foundation, created by James Rouse, has attempted an holistic approach to uplifting entire families, neighbors, and whole blocks of people, in one of the worst neighborhoods in Baltimore, by utilizing a wide variety of assistance in family planning, job training, drug counseling, and similar activities. Although major improvements in living conditions have been accomplished, lack of funds, jobs, and Black political leadership have hampered real success.

Many cities have been nibbling away at the worst cores of their inner city neighborhoods by locating public facilities or encouraging private housing or mixed use developments, usually with a small percentage of units reserved for low to moderate income individuals or families. These techniques, plus the use of Section 8 vouchers, tend to move out some of the poorest people in the neighborhoods. Since available Section 8 apartments are typically clustered, that process simply moves the social-economic problems to a different location. Those tactics have little chance of making the old neighborhoods desirable places to live or in which to do business.

In his landmark book focusing on these problems, *Inside Game/ Outside Game*, Urban Strategist David Rusk, using decades of research, declares that only a metropolitan-wide community effort and funding will eventually save the people in the worst neighborhood from more generations of poverty and misery. He also blames urban sprawl around hemmed-in cities for the failure to join regional efforts to deal with that crisis. His concepts of tax-sharing make great sense but cannot be accomplished without enlightened state and regional leadership.

His brilliant analysis of the troubled City of Baltimore entitled, *Baltimore Unbound*, is a masterpiece of understanding and intelligent urban medicine. Its holistic recommendations have been ignored.

Only by taking the left fork in the road and embracing three key policies for the urban growth of our metropolitan cities can we create the living conditions we want our grandchildren to experience.

Recommended National Policies on Urban Growth

It shall be the policy of the United States Government to lead, assist, and provide incentives to metropolitan areas toward a higher level of formal cooperation and unified planning and activities to maximize the benefits of coming urban growth.

Every year, billions of dollars are granted to cities, counties, and states to improve the quality of life in their areas. Only in rare cases are there federal mandates requiring cooperative and unified planning, particularly in transportation and environmental controls and management.

A new criterion will be introduced in the evaluation of proposed funding for all federal programs affecting metropolitan areas that will favor those that show affirmative progress toward regional management of urban programs. Federal grants will be made to assist in restructuring local governments aimed at consolidation or through the creation of permanent intergovernmental compacts.

1. No center city should be shouldered with the sole responsibility of erasing their blighted and dangerous neighborhoods. One of the most critical goals in the field of governmental reform will be the utilization of regional resources including planning, leadership, and funding toward the broad sharing of responsibilities for the creative improvement of individual and family lives in those areas. Through "holistic caring" about those Americans trapped in dangerous neighborhoods, close attention must be directed to assist those living in substandard housing, those needing intensive counseling and by integrating support programs toward uplifting the quality of life as well as the physical environment.

2. Each metropolitan area whose local governments, directly or indirectly, receive federal funds will be encouraged to recognize and measure the human, social, and financial costs of the continued spreading out of community development. Each area will be called upon to devise its own best methodology for achieving the unified capacity to determine areas suitable for development and those areas to be preserved from development.

To effectuate these national policies on Urban Growth, Congress will be called upon to create a new *National Partnership for MetroCities* to serve as the managers of these proposed policies. This non-profit corporation will manage the described programs in the public interest. It will have the powers of a governmental agency but be organized to operate as private company. It will obtain the majority of its eventual funding from private investors but will cooperate closely with the Congress on a matching system in order to support the most costly activities already funded by the legislative branch. The President and the Congress will appoint the members of the Board of Directors of the *Partnership*.

The ultimate goals of these policies are to change the direction of urban growth in the United States. Nothing in these concepts is aimed to stifle growth in smaller cities or outlying areas that may not require massive federal expenditures due to the lesser impact of that growth. Among its main purposes is the prevention of large city/regions from becoming unmanageable mega-cities as are rising throughout the world.

To our heirs we will bequeath center cities and their suburban neighbors that will be free of slums, vibrant in their urban activities, and capable of controlling their outer boundaries. This equilibrium will allow the installation of transportation systems geared toward moving people not cars. The skies will be clear as will streams and rivers.

Let us hope that, by 2035, we will treat newcomers as friends and neighbors and have organized the institutions of education and-recreation to help them to grow in their new home nation. As they have for over 200 years, migrants will become a population engine of growth and service.

Observation
What's So Special About Portland?

Once you get over the soggy weather and the rarity of bright sunny days, Portland, OR, looks and feels like a model city. Portland is Oregon's largest metropolitan area and has an international reputation for its growth management policies. It has become a living laboratory for forward thinking urban planning and action. Certain conditions existed in the area that led to progressive political actions that resulted in its national leadership.

The reasons given were a relatively homogeneous and young population, a lack of old-fashioned political machines, a tradition of policy innovation, and the fact that its urban population had a connection with the forested open spaces for recreation and aesthetic enjoyment. Also, the state had already exercised some controls over municipal planning and zoning so that a regional planning and management entity might give them more say on regional matters.

In planning circles, Portland is best known for its Urban Growth Boundary. It surrounds twenty-four cities, parts of three Counties and a little more than 1.3 million people. Planners would argue that the boundary has lessened urban sprawl and slowed growth, but objectors complain that it has caused the elevation of housing prices and dampened private development. The Portland region is also well known for its 1986 light rail system including a major extension in 1998. Transit-oriented development has resulted in high density housing near stations toward improving ridership.

The Portland area has the only directly elected regional government in the United States. Although local communities retained planning and zoning responsibilities, their plans must conform to the regional plan and related controls. The Metro government has many functions that include conservation, open space acquisition and operations, and managing the zoo, the Oregon Convention Center, and the Portland Center for the Performing Arts.

Faced with the prospect of a projected 700,000 new residents and over 300,000 new jobs, the Metro planners recently proposed a 2040 Growth Concept that featured a pattern of strong sub-centers and an extended multi-modal transportation system. It also strongly recommended small lot subdivisions and minimum densities in the cities and counties toward reducing sprawl. They also adopted many of the principles of the New Urbanism.

In 1995, the voters approved a $136 million bond issue to buy 8,000 acres of open space. In 2006, they approved a $277 million bond issue to purchase approximately 4,000 acres of additional open space, dedicated $44 million to local governments to protect natural areas and water quality, and set aside $15 million for "Nature in Neighborhoods." There has been some criticism of the acquisition program because many of the lands purchased are too far out to serve the existing population.

Observation
Guess Who's Building a Petroleum-free Town?

It is easy to get confused about those little oil-rich countries on the Persian Gulf. They seem like little cousins to Saudi Arabia, the big dog in the region, but mile-for-mile, the little Emirates have more oil than you know who! Their leaders, Sheiks with degrees from Oxford and MIT, are ambitious business leaders who, like the Saudis, own their own country and everything under it.

They are building the world's tallest buildings and clusters of masterpiece museums and universities as cultural and educational showplaces and resource buildings for the next generations. Their own people do not do menial work, so the vast majority of true workers are foreigners with no permanent homes or rights.

But the inventive Sheiks control the funds so they can build whatever they want wherever they want. Building permits, ha! They are also in the race for bragging right on several fronts among the other sheikdoms. The only seven-star hotel in the world is in Dubai! Where?

To one-up his equals in the wonderland of fabulous structures and luxury appointments, little but super-rich Abu Dhabi has announced the first carbon-neutral 2,400-acre "city." It will be powered by the sun, the wind, and geo-thermal energy and no automobiles as we know them will be allowed within the walls of this settlement.

The so-called experiment has attracted development partners like British Petroleum, Fiat, General Electric, and Mitsubishi. Their scientists are expected to contribute greatly to the design and construction of this miraculous new place.

MIT is helping them build the Masdar Institute to offer masters and doctorates in science and engineering. The eyes of the world will be on this island of idealism!

Chapter 11.
A Timetable for Action

This timetable is offered not so much as an idealistic dream of what will really happen but as a sequenced guideline for people to think about. The only way it could be realistic is if a forward-thinking President and an eager and cooperative Congress would embrace these concepts and proceed with them or some similar scenario.

Spring 2009: The new President would lead the Nation into a posture of world leadership by offering a twenty-year International Job Corps that would operate like the Peace Corps but would also assist in capital formation for new plants, recruiting, and training the unemployed with financial assistance during that long-term process. A similar U.S. training program would be launched to break the cycle of poverty, unemployment, and disrupted family life in America's central cities.

Fall 2009: Congress would hold hearings on and pass the bill to create the *National Partnership for MetroCities* and authorize the first funds to launch the program for regional and metropolitan cooperation aimed at new coalitions preparing to take advantage of the new incentives. The *Partnership* would be authorized to serve as the conduit for matching funding for existing cities, to locate the first new MetroCity, and to issue the first phase of its revenue bonds to finance that venture.

Spring 2011: The *Partnership* would have received and approved twenty-one proposals from metropolitan areas containing a wide variety of ingenious structures for working together on major common problems, many of which did not even include transportation or utilities. The concept of "holistic caring" would have been embraced by most of the applicants.

Fall 2012: The *Partnership* announces that, after reviewing several potential sites for the first new MetroCity, one had passed the rigorous testing including the feasibility of acquiring over 60,000 acres in one general location. The exact location would be announced early in 2013.

Spring 2013: The first new MetroCity site was identified in central Pennsylvania, more or less halfway between Philadelphia and Pittsburgh. It is expected to draw considerable growth from the Philadelphia coastal area and provide generations of new jobs for the local population.

Fall 2013: A second site for a new MetroCity on the border between California and Nevada has been chosen. The site is a 50,000 acre valley surrounded by 9,000 ft. peaks.

The National Partnership for MetroCities announced that over $500 million has been granted to metropolitan areas that have made remarkable progress in dealing with a myriad of social problems in their areas and many have decided on an Urban Growth Boundary even though it is unpopular in many local regions.

Spring 2020: Over thirty of the largest metro areas in the Nation have applied and become eligible for *National Partnership* funding and all have focused on the human and physical renewal of their central city, a regional mechanism for problem solving, and many more have proposed Urban Growth Boundaries to control sprawl.

All eight new MetroCities are underway, each of which are close to the 64,000 acre target, each planned for over 200,000 dwelling units and most are showing extraordinary expansion in job creation and the development of new institutions designed to promote the promise of the new communities.

In all cases, hundreds of companies have been formed or relocated to the new sites where a lifetime of opportunities present themselves and permanent employment is all but assured as is life in an innovative and pollution-free environment.

Needless to say, such a massive building program has had problems with lawsuits, recalcitrant neighbors, no-growth advocates, and government bureaucracy. Nevertheless, the MetroCities move forward, meeting their goals for whole new ways of city life, relieving pressures on older areas, and directing community development profits to help those older cities. In 2030, the twenty-year American experiment will be reviewed and tested. It is our fond hope that the applause will have been earned.

Observation
Water, Water Everywhere...But at What Price?

The term "Aquifer" refers to a massive, natural, underground river that flows endlessly in a specified geographic area. The Floridan aquifer system runs under about 100,000 square miles in southern Alabama, southeastern Georgia, southern South Carolina, and all of Florida. It provides water for Jacksonville, Orlando, Tallahassee, and St. Petersburg.

It also provides gushing supplies for Savannah, GA. However, one of its suburban cities, Rincon, a rapidly growing jurisdiction has increased its population to 7,000 from 4,400 in 1996. That is not a dramatic number but a combination of residential and industrial growth has put a heavy demand on its dubious water supply at the far limits of the Floridan aquifer.

The community has been warned that in the near future their wells will be contaminated by salt water and be useless for drinking or irrigation. The little town has spent over $13 million to build a plant to reuse water for lawns and golf courses. People who have moved from Savannah to find more affordable housing are now experiencing water bills of $300 a month up from $30.

Even the Chamber of Commerce's chief executive has expressed concern over the pace of growth; there is no community-wide opposition to continued development. Both the Federal government and the State of Georgia have warned Rincon and its neighboring areas that salt water intrusion is on the way. The common view is, "we'll just have to pay more for good water."

Observation
Pedaling Your Way to the Sights

What do Stockholm, Copenhagen, Barcelona, Brussels, Vienna, and Paris have in common? They all have huge rent-a-bike programs, but Paris has outdone them all by launching 750 "Help Yourself" rental stations with over 10,000 new bikes! Just swipe your credit card through the small computer and away you go!

Paris now has 230 miles of bike lanes, but watch out for the auto and bus drivers; they have not lost their spirit. Biking is cheap, too. A daily pass is $1.36 and a seven-day ticket is only $6.80, the price of an average glass of wine. When ready to rent, press your choice of eight languages and instructions will come forth. Each bike has a basket and a lock. Bring your own helmet or buy one at a bike shop.

There are a few limitations. The renter-rider must be fourteen or up and be at least five feet tall. There are no baby seats yet. The new service started in July, 2007.

For more information, See www.velib.parisfr. Which American city will be first? Bikes away!

Chapter 12.
The Year 2000 Plan for the Nation's Capital

This document was prepared by the staffs of the National Capital Planning Commission and the National Capital Regional Planning Commission from mid-1959 to the Spring of 1961, headed by William E. Finley, Director of NCPC. At that time, the Washington region was the fastest growing metropolitan area in the nation. Its population was approximately two million and projected by the planners to reach five million by the Year 2000. It did.

After examining many alternative potential growth concepts, both the Planning Commission and the Regional Planning Commission adopted the Radial Corridor Plan that envisioned six development corridors anchored by new towns on a rail transit line and interstate highways. The corridors would be separated by broad wedges of very low-density development and permanently protected open space.

The Washington Metropolitan Regional Conference consisting of elected representatives from Maryland and Virginia and District of Columbia Commissioners embraced the Radial Corridor Plan and recommended it to the local governments in the region.

On May 6th, 1961, President Kennedy signed the document and forwarded the Plan to all branches of the United States government involved in the Capital area and urged their serious considerations. On November 27, 1962, the President issued an Executive Order instructing all agencies of the Executive Branch and the District government declaring that the Plan was the approved policy document "as the basic development scheme for the National Capital Region."

The various regional development concepts examined in *The Year 2000 Plan* may be of interest to regional planning bodies in the 21st Century.

THE WHITE HOUSE
WASHINGTON

May 8, 1961

TO THE PEOPLE OF THE NATIONAL CAPITAL REGION

From the days of L'Enfant, Americans have come to expect the best of their Nation's Capital. More than any other city -- more than any other region, the Nation's Capital should represent the finest in a living environment which America can plan and build.

The actions that will be taken in the years ahead by the governmental jurisdictions of the area and by the Federal departments and agencies will have a major effect on the welfare of the area's residents, and the status of Washington as the Nation's Capital.

The development policies recommended in the Year 2000 Plan Report prepared by the National Capital Planning Commission and the National Capital Regional Planning Council are worthy of consideration by all who are concerned with the future character and quality of the Federal City and its environs.

ABOUT THIS REPORT

With two million people, the National Capital Region is one of the Nation's ten largest metropolitan areas.

It is a good place to live and do business. It is a fine setting for our Nation's Capital.

But, like every metropolis, it has problems—traffic congestion, water pollution, vanishing open space, crowded schools, rising taxes, obsolescence, blight. These problems are steadily getting more serious, despite the determined efforts of many people.

Why? The main reason is *growth*. People keep coming to Washington, and the people who are already here keep having children. The Region's population will double within a generation through natural increase alone. This means more building, more cars on the streets, more children going to school, more water consumed, more people using the parks and playgrounds. Growth means more people making more demands on a limited amount of land, on limited amounts of water and air, on public facilities that can only be expanded slowly and at considerable cost, and on public revenues that never seem to grow as fast as the need for them.

What kind of a place will the National Capital Region be in the years to come? Will it meet the needs of its greatly increased population, of the many people who visit it each year, and of the Federal government whose headquarters is here? Or will we still be struggling with the problems that bother us today, as well as with entirely new ones?

The answer to these questions depends, to a considerable extent, on the Region's *pattern of growth*—the direction in which growth occurs; the extent to which it is concentrated or dispersed; the proportion of industry, shopping, and various kinds of housing in each part of the Region; the location of open spaces and centers of intensive development; the arrangement of new Federal buildings and monuments; the location of the growing highway and transit network; the layout of individual business districts and residential areas.

Our future depends, in a word, on the *design* of the Region—on the creation of a pattern of growth that will produce the best possible environment for ourselves and future generations. Good design will reduce traffic congestion, protect water supplies, provide adequate space for parks and recreation, create efficient commercial centers and livable residential neighborhoods, produce a suitable setting for the Nation's Capital, meet the needs of new industry, and reduce the costs of local government. Good design will give us delight in the visual quality of our urban environment. Poor design will increase the cost, frustration and visual chaos that each of us experiences in working and living at close quarters with several million other people.

Many people can help to design a larger and better metropolis—businessmen deciding to build new office buildings and shopping centers, corporations choosing sites for new plants, builders planning new subdivisions and redevelopment projects. But many of the most important decisions are in the hands of the governments of the Region. The Federal government builds office buildings and laboratories, airports and parkways; the States and the District of Columbia build highways and bridges; the local governments build schools, water and sewage works, and many other public works. The local governments also regulate building and the use of land by private owners. All governments buy, hold, and occasionally dispose of considerable quantities of land.

The future of the Region therefore depends, in great measure, on the way in which the governments of the Region shape its growth—on the design objectives they set for the Region, and on the way they carry out that design. This will be a lengthy and complex process. It can only succeed if the many detailed decisions that shape the Region's growth are guided by basic long-range policies which aim at the realization of a sound regional design. This report is a first step in the process of formulating a design and technique for shaping regional development.

Toward a consensus cooperatively arrived at, this report offers the following for the consideration of the public officials and the citizens of the Region:

1. A forward look at the prospective growth of the Region and its consequences.

2. A statement of goals to serve as a basis for policies on regional development.

3. An evaluation of alternative patterns of regional growth, and a recommendation in favor of a pattern that seems both to hold the greatest promise and to be possible of achievement.

4. A set of recommended policies to guide governmental decisions in the direction of a sound design of the entire Region and each of its parts. Separate policies are proposed for the Region, for the District of Columbia, and for the all-important core where governmental and business activities are heavily concentrated—Metro-Center.

5. A description of the next steps that should be taken in deciding upon and carrying out policies for regional development.

The result is not a detailed plan for the physical development of the Region, but rather a set of policies to guide governmental decision-making and the preparation of physical plans. The aim is to inaugurate a process of openly arrived at decision and action which will shape the Region in the years to come.

This report is being submitted to each of the government agencies that make fundamental decisions in shaping the Region's growth—the governing body of each county and city, the Board of Commissioners of the District of Columbia, the Governors of Maryland and Virginia, the various Federal agencies, and the committees on the District of Columbia of the two houses of Congress. It is hoped that each agency and official will carefully and constructively consider the policies recommended herein, and that all will join in a cooperative effort to design and create a National Capital Region worthy of a great nation and fully adequate to the needs of the millions who will be living in the Region or visiting it in the years to come.

This report is also being published and distributed widely throughout the Region, to alert the citizens and civic leaders to the decisions facing them and their public officials. It is hoped that there will be a widespread, thorough and constructive public discussion of the issues raised in this report and the recommendations offered herein.

A PROSPECTUS FOR THE NATIONAL CAPITAL REGION

GROWTH

The Region is growing rapidly, and there is every evidence that it will continue to do so. The population increased by 37 percent, reaching two million, during the past decade; it could easily reach five million by the Year 2000. This concentration of population in a great metropolis can result in a better life—or in a more difficult one—for all who live here, depending upon what is done to fit the additional millions onto a limited amount of land. The question, therefore, is not "if" the Region will grow, but how much, in what direction, and to what purpose.

ALTERNATIVES

Urban growth patterns are no longer narrowly restrained by their dependence upon the location of raw materials, port facilities, and rail transportation. A metropolis can now choose to grow in any one of a variety of ways. Rising productivity contributes to this effect, since we can now build and rebuild much more rapidly and extensively than was dreamed of in earlier years. Rich new possibilities are thus opened up to the metropolitan region which considers alternatives before choosing to guide growth in a preferred direction.

A KIT OF TOOLS

New tools of design are being created continually. Several are still being styled, including urban renewal and measures to preserve open space. Others, such as zoning, subdivision control, and reservation of land for parks and highways, need sharpening. Used in concert, the means within our reach can shape the Region and each of its parts into the form we desire.

NEEDED: REGIONAL AGREEMENT

The successful use of these tools depends upon the degree to which the people of the Region unite around a single set of development policies. The formation of the Washington Metropolitan Regional Conference demonstrates that the area's top political leaders see each county and city as a part of a single interdependent metropolitan community, and that each can prosper best by cooperation with its neighbor. The other levels of government—Federal and State—also recognize that it is in their own interest to strengthen the united approach to the development of the Nation's Capital and its Metropolitan Region.

POLICIES FOR THE YEAR 2000

The recommended policies *reject:*

Uncontrolled urban sprawl as a pattern of new development;

A congested or declining central city;

The wasteful destruction of the countryside; but also

Metropolitan development forms which will require unacceptable controls to accomplish.

This statement of policies *recommends:*

The creation of relatively compact, well-planned suburban communities;

The concentration of the new communities in corridors radiating from the central city;

Greater reliance on mass transportation;

Limiting the freeway system largely to the routes already planned;

Growth of the employment concentration in Metro-Center, but with two thirds of all new Federal employment being located elsewhere within the Region;

The renewal of most of the original City of Washington;

No increase in population within the District of Columbia, but the attainment of quality and individuality for each of its communities;

The reservation of major portions of the countryside as permanent open space; and

Steps that can be taken to implement the above recommendations within the present framework of government and with means available or in the making.

A FORTY-YEAR PERSPECTIVE

While there is an urgent need for a prompt start on this process, some of its effects will not be felt for years. The guiding policies must look far beyond the near future, which will largely be shaped by decisions already made, to a time when needs and conditions are different from today. An attempt has been made to anticipate the Region's character more than a generation hence, and to formulate policies that will be appropriate to the end of the century. This is a report, then, on policies for the Year 2000.

The forty-year period has been chosen because over such a long period of time great changes are sure to take place, and these changes can be very greatly influenced by public policies.

ROLES OF NCPC AND NCRPC

The Congress of the United States in 1952 re-created the NCPC as "The central planning agency for the Federal and District governments to plan the appropriate and orderly development and redevelopment of the National Capital. . . ."

At the same time, the NCRPC was created to prepare a general plan for the development of the National Capital Region and to promote collaboration and cooperation between the Commission and the planning agencies of the environs.

It is, therefore, fitting that these two agencies jointly propose development policies for the Federal City and the Region.

A SPECIAL REGION

As the seat of the National Government, this Region is called upon to perform specialized functions and has special needs. The symbolic beauty of the buildings and monuments along the Mall is admired by visitors from all over the world and constant vigilance is needed to protect it. The City about it should be of equal quality—as should the Region as a whole. New development, both inside the District and in the rest of the Region, should embody the specially high standards of quality befitting a great capital. These standards should be reflected in the design of whole communities as well as individual buildings, in landscaping and the management of parks and open lands, and in the construction of highways and other public works.

The recommended policies would inject quality in three major areas:

1. IN METRO-CENTER, the heart of the nation's capital city, by assuring greater strength and vitality.

2. IN SUBURBAN DEVELOPMENT CORRIDORS where the highest level of design and community facilities can serve the great numbers of new residents.

3. And, for the benefit of all the Region's people IN THE OPEN COUNTRY BETWEEN THE CORRIDORS OF GROWTH. The basic quality of the region will be greatly affected by the amount and nature of the lands held OUT of development, as well as by the development that takes place.

THE PAST IS PROLOGUE

This statement of policies builds on the achievements of the past. In the 170 years since it was founded, Washington has become a great world capital. Many people have helped to establish its present form. From L'Enfant forward, even during the century of neglect ending in 1901, great leaders have pressed for improvements—always with some vision in mind. The leading image of the past —*the monumental city*—is no longer adequate by itself. The monumental city is today surrounded by a growing expanse of new urban development. Today, a more complex goal must be sought—that of a careful and happy marriage of the symbolic and aesthetic values of the monumental city with the diversified functions of the nation's capital city and a great metropolitan region.

This report is intended to be a start toward the creation of a much larger image—*a National Capital Region*—which reflects the accomplishments of the past and the promise of the future.

NEXT STEPS

The NCPC hopes to receive constructive comments on the various policies as they may affect the location of Federal facilities, the rebuilding of older portions of the city, the location of freeways and rapid transit lines and stations and many other matters.

The NCRPC is ready to work with each of the local governments in the Region to evaluate the policies recommended herein, and to assess their implications for local planning and development programs.

The Commission and Council hope to adopt a Year 2000 Plan during 1961, applying the policies recommended in this report. Such a plan would represent Federal policy on the development of the Region, and would serve as a guide to local development decisions wherever appropriate.

The Commission and Council will also proceed with further studies and evaluation of the recommended policies, to provide additional information on which to base their consideration.

POPULATION: THE EXPLOSION

The well-publicized "population explosion" is as much a prospect for the United States as it is for the rest of the world: if present trends continue, our population will almost double by the Year 2000. This means that we will have the same numerical growth in the next forty years that we have had in the last two centuries.

Almost all of this growth will take place in metropolitan areas. This will be a continuation of a long-term trend. In 1850, only fifteen percent of our population lived in urban areas; today that proportion approaches seventy percent. The number of metropolitan areas containing more than 100,000 people has grown from 52 in 1900 to 193 in 1960, and could number 300 by the Year 2000 if present trends continue.

Most of the growth of the metropolitan areas has taken place in and beyond what we now describe as "the suburbs," for well known reasons: near-capacity residential densities in the central cities, mass ownership of the automobile, the availability of new types of home financing, the use of mass-building techniques. These and related circumstances will surely continue to produce massive growth outside the District of Columbia during the decades ahead.

THE ECONOMY: MORE EXPANSION

Economic trends will have an important influence on the development of every metropolitan area.

PRODUCTIVITY

Possible increases in the productivity of the average worker are indicated by a recent Twentieth Century Fund report on needs and resources, which states ". . . the average rate of increase over the past century would yield fabulous results if long continued. By 2050 we would be able to produce and earn as much in one seven-hour day as we do now in a forty-hour week, and as we did in 1850, working for more than three weeks at seventy hours a week."

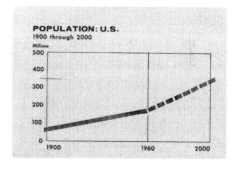

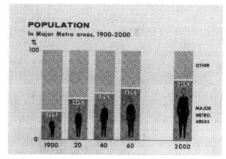

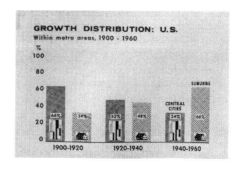

WORK FORCE

Recent studies indicate that there will be very little change in the size of the work force as a proportion of total population by the Year 2000, though there may be appreciable changes in its composition. For example, proportions for some male age groups will probably decline because more years will be spent at school and because retirement will be earlier. This will be balanced by increases in the proportion of working wives, a trend which has been noticeable for some time.

EDUCATION

The work force will be much better educated. In 1940, the average number of years of schooling of workers between the ages of 18 and 64 was 9.3; by 1950 the average had risen to 12.0. It is predicted that this ratio will increase until seven out of ten young workers entering the labor force in the 1960's will have a high-school education or better.

EMPLOYMENT TYPE

Although nearly every type of employment in the economy is expected to grow, rates of growth will be substantially higher for some types than for others. Highest growth rates are anticipated in government, wholesale and retail trade, services, and finance. Above-average increases are going to be experienced, in short, by the white-collar occupations (professional, technical, clerical, and sales) and among service workers, while somewhat lower growth rates are in prospect for the blue-collar groups (craftsmen, operatives, and laborers). Actual declines are ahead for farmers and farm laborers.

INCOME AND THE WORK WEEK

The worker of the future will spend fewer hours at work each week, and his purchasing power will continue to increase.

To summarize, the general trend points to an economy which will give everyone more time to spend more money for more goods and services. The kinds of goods and services the consumer will be buying in the Year 2000 is subject to much speculation, since probably more than half of the kinds of products which will be on the market in 2000 are not even in existence today. Present tendencies indicate relatively smaller outlays for such necessities as food, clothing, and housing, and more for recreation, education and labor-saving devices.

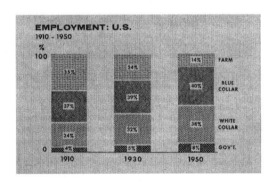

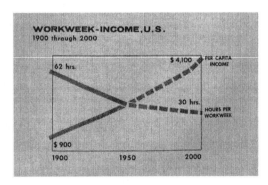

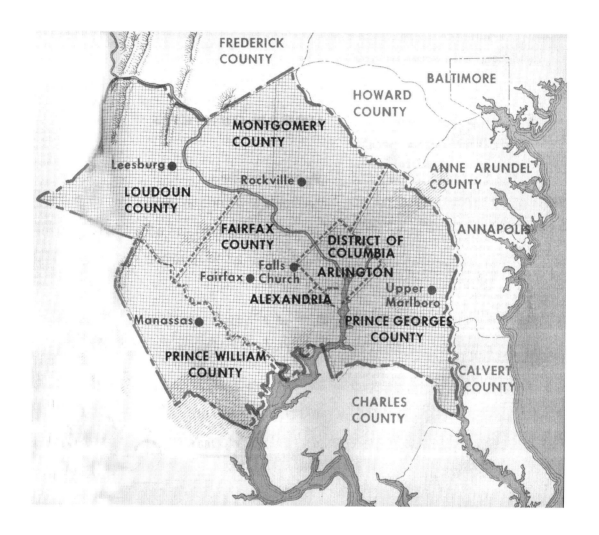

PROJECTIONS FOR THE LAND

Growth within the National Capital Region has brought with it all of the problems of change—mushrooming subdivisions with their new demands for public services, the decline of older neighborhoods, more traffic, higher costs of doing business. Meanwhile, local governments have been too preoccupied with meeting day-to-day needs to consider how to alter the on-going pattern of development. No let-up in the pace of growth is in sight, as Washington becomes more tightly woven into the urban fabric of the Eastern seaboard. There is, therefore, an urgent need to consider some basic issues about the way in which the Region is to grow.

How should this new urban growth be distributed on the land? This is the basic issue to be faced in framing land development policies for the decades ahead. Most of us are familiar with what has been happening to the land during the past years of growth. If these low-density development patterns continue, this metropolis will spread over an area five times its present size by the Year 2000, extending from Leesburg and Manassas to the shores of the Chesapeake, and from the Frederick County line into the middle of Charles County.

RESIDENTIAL LAND

In this metropolitan area, as in all metropolitan areas, suburban growth in recent decades has occurred typically through a process of "scatteration" and "leap-frogging" as new subdivisions have been built beyond closer-in undeveloped land. For the people living in the new communities, the costs of this process are mounting—in daily travel requirements, in extended utility systems, in the burden of maintaining acceptable levels of public service. Those living in the central parts of the metropolitan area, on the other hand, are having to go farther and farther out to enjoy really open countryside.

THE ISSUE: How can the timing of development and the layout of new communities be regulated to achieve the economies of more efficient land use?

Even aside from "leap-frogging," the new suburbs use land more extravagantly than the older communities. Each 1,000 inhabitants of the outer suburbs today use about 200 acres for homes and neighborhood facilities, compared to an average of only 70 acres for the same number of people in the previously built-up area. While the new suburban residents appear to be willing to pay the costs of this type of development, they might not be if they had suitable alternatives to choose from. In any case, there will be an increased demand for higher density development as the suburban economy diversifies and its population gains an increasing share of young adults and elderly people.

While low-density scatteration is typical of the outer suburbs, the older residential sections in the District of Columbia and a few of the older suburban areas are suffering from advanced age and neglect. Every year, an-other portion of this older housing becomes obsolescent. The Region's lower-income population can find little housing except in these inner deteriorated areas, though the decentralization of economic activity is steadily creating new jobs for this population outside the District of Columbia. Conversely, most of the middle- and upper-income population can find acceptable housing only in the suburbs, though a large proportion of this population is employed in Metro-Center. As a result, the choice of housing open to all income groups is limited, and tremendous demands are created for rush-hour transportation between suburb and city.

THE ISSUE: How can the central city and the older suburbs be preserved, renewed, and redeveloped to provide suitable housing opportunities for all segments of the population, thereby extending the scope of choice and reducing rush-hour traffic problems?

THE ISSUE: How should land-use plans for new suburbs recognize from the start eventual needs for a variety of housing types in each suburban community, reserving the proper land at the outset for higher density land uses?

OPEN SPACE

A metropolis needs many kinds of open space for many different purposes: for recreation, for conservation of natural resources, for preservation of scenic beauty. For a growing metropolis, the essential open space problem is summed up in the simple fact that, as the demand for open space increases, the supply nearest at hand is consumed at an accelerated rate.

The amount of land needed for recreation, for example, has been increasing at a compounded rate from the combined effects of increases in population, in leisure time, in average income, and in mobility. The developing suburban communities find it extremely difficult to acquire needed park lands in the face of their many other immediate financial problems. Also, land costs continue to rise, so that each dollar spent buys less land than before.

THE ISSUE: How can sufficient land to meet future public recreation needs be acquired or dedicated in the proper places in time to prevent loss of the land to other urban uses?

The necessity for keeping the Region's rivers and streams clean requires no argument. The measures required to control run-off from the watersheds feeding these streams can also serve other purposes, particularly recreation.

THE ISSUE: Wherein does concern for protecting the Region's water supply suggest specific programs for the preservation of countryside surrounding the metropolis?

A city is not a completely man-made environment. Many of the living things in a city exist only with man's permission and maintenance. Yet cities are carved out of open lands that once had their own natural ecological balance. Enough of this natural condition should be preserved in every metropolitan area for the enlightenment and enjoyment of its future citizens.

THE ISSUE: How can the appropriate lands be acquired and preserved in a natural state?

THE CITY AND ITS SUBURBS ARE INTERDEPENDENT PARTS OF A SINGLE COMMUNITY, BOUND TOGETHER BY A WEB OF TRANSPORTATION AND OTHER PUBLIC FACILITIES AND BY COMMON ECONOMIC INTERESTS. BOLD PROGRAMS IN INDIVIDUAL JURISDICTIONS ARE NO LONGER ENOUGH. INCREASINGLY, COMMUNITY DEVELOPMENT MUST BE A COOPERATIVE VENTURE THROUGH THE COMMON GOALS OF THE METROPOLITAN REGION AS A WHOLE.

THIS REQUIRES THE ESTABLISHMENT OF AN EFFECTIVE AND COMPREHENSIVE PLANNING PROCESS IN EACH METROPOLITAN AREA EMBRACING ALL MAJOR ACTIVITIES, BOTH PUBLIC AND PRIVATE, WHICH SHAPE THE COMMUNITY. SUCH A PROCESS MUST BE DEMOCRATIC—FOR ONLY WHEN THE CITIZENS OF A COMMUNITY HAVE PARTICIPATED IN SELECTING THE GOALS WHICH WILL SHAPE THEIR ENVIRONMENT CAN THEY BE EXPECTED TO SUPPORT THE ACTIONS NECESSARY TO ACCOMPLISH THESE GOALS.

(FROM PRESIDENT KENNEDY'S SPECIAL MESSAGE TO CONGRESS ON HOUSING AND COMMUNITY DEVELOPMENT, MARCH 9, 1961)

PART V NCR POLICIES PLAN | 34

NCR: BASIC POLICIES

The National Capital Region should prepare to accommodate a population growth up to a total of five million by the Year 2000.

The governments of the Region can encourage or discourage population growth to some extent. State and local governments can do so by encouraging or discouraging new industry, while the Federal Government can do so by increasing or decreasing the number of its employees located here.

Federal policy for many years has been to decentralize all functions that can well be located elsewhere. Some local governments have worked in the opposite direction, making considerable efforts to attract new industry. While these efforts can produce some increase in the rate of growth, and a contrary policy of discouraging industry could retard rate of growth to some extent, the most important influences on the growth of new industry will be the presence of a local mass market and the Region's attractiveness to scientific and technical organizations.

The only governmental policy that might cause the population to grow much more rapidly than has been predicted would be a massive increase in Federal employment here, which seems neither desirable nor likely, barring a serious change in the international situation.

A substantially slower rate of growth might be considered desirable by some. Policies to limit growth are entirely conceivable, and are in fact currently being applied within at least two of the world's great metropolitan areas: Tokyo (ten million), and Moscow (eleven million).

In order to restrict the growth of the National Capital Region, it would be necessary for the local governments to limit severely the land available to new industry; to acquire large amounts of land for a greenbelt around the urbanized area, preventing its outward growth; and to control rigorously the density of development within the urbanized area. Even with such policies in effect, a substantial amount of growth would take place. The result would be a metropolitan area considerably larger than it is today, but developing in a pattern similar to that of the recent past (see RESTRICTED GROWTH diagram).

RESTRICTED GROWTH

 urbanized area

• sub-center

 controlled open space

↔↔ main communication lines

NATIONAL CAPITAL REGION

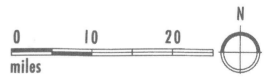

0   10   20   N

miles

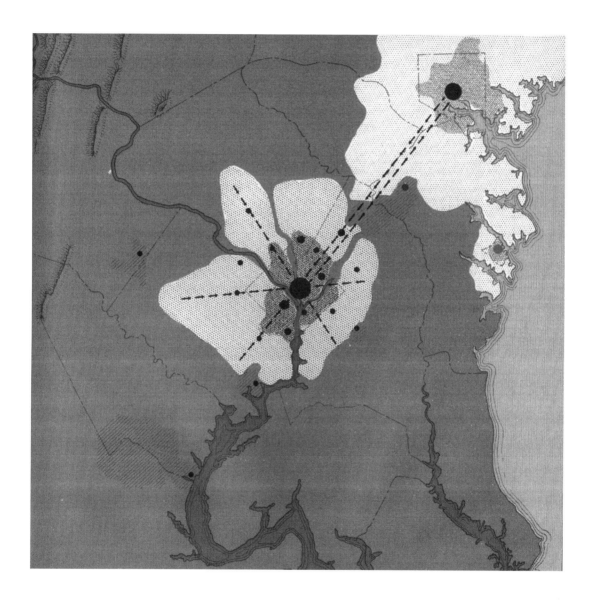

The final alternative (RADIAL CORRIDOR PLAN) profits from consideration of all the previous four. The greater part of the Region's growth would still be accommodated in new communities. Just as in three of the previous alternatives, each of the new urban areas would offer a broad range of housing types, and development density would be somewhat higher than is typical of today's suburban areas. Each would contain important centers of employment and commercial activity providing a high degree of local self-sufficiency. But in this case, the new communities would develop in corridors radiating outward from the center of the Region.

This pattern of regional development offers clear and decisive advantages over each of the others. By concentrating development along radial corridors, it offers the greatest opportunity to exploit the carrying potential of mass transportation. Its radial pattern permits especially efficient access to the central city provided conflicts between local and through traffic can be avoided by design. The employment center at the core of the Region would therefore have a potential for growth not possible under any other arrangement. Every part of the Region would have ready access to the variety of employment opportunity and social interchange available in the Region. Furthermore, the areas lying between the development corridors would provide significant stretches of open countryside penetrating the urban area as wedges readily accessible to the whole population, yet far enough out of the path of development to facilitate their preservation in open use. This approach to regional development is, therefore, seen as offering the highest promise as a guide to the growth of the National Capital Region during the decades ahead.

THE RADIAL CORRIDOR PLAN

 new town center

 urbanized area

● **sub-center**

 controlled open space

→← **main communication lines**

NATIONAL CAPITAL REGION

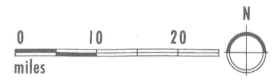

0   10   20   N

miles

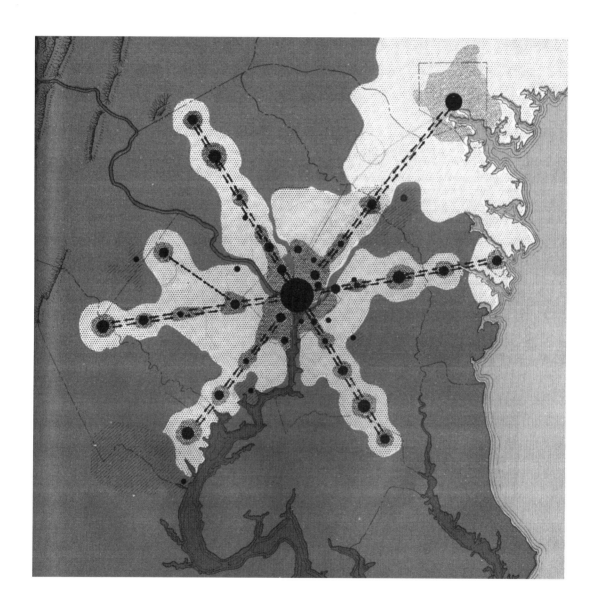

Chapter 13.
The New South Richmond Project

Late in 1968, the then Mayor of New York City, the progressive Republican John V. Lindsay, having heard of the successful launching of Columbia, MD, the new town created by James Rouse and his associates, approached Rouse with a challenge. He described the southern one-third of Staten Island, the fifth borough of the City, historically named South Richmond.

The lower one-third, approximately 12,000 acres (Columbia was 14,000 acres) was largely empty, had 12,500 individual parcels of which the City owned 3,000 in addition to many acres of "paper" streets. The vacant lands and beaches were strewn with junk and a variety of wildlife played amidst the debris.

The Rouse Company's consulting subsidiary, the American City Corporation, headed by Leo Molinaro, was asked to consider a wide choice of development options since there were no standing policies other than, on occasion, to allow a house on the typical 40-foot lot, although there were few water lines and no sanitary sewers in the area.

The team produced a monument of analyses and clearly stated community development scenarios, recommended the middle density model, and produced public and private development financial models based on the Columbia experience.

The report, presented in May 1970 was heralded in the press and well received by Governor Nelson Rockefeller, Mayor Lindsay, the Borough President, and a majority of Staten island political leaders. The local State Senator introduced the bill into the New York State Senate to create the entity to redevelop the South Richmond area.

The proposed organization was modeled after the then very active New York State Urban Development Corporation. The bill passed the State Senate but was stalled in the State House of Representatives by an enemy of Mayor Lindsay. Neither Rockefeller, the Mayor, nor the Borough President could remove the blockage. The bill was reintroduced the next year but was still buried by the State House.

Mayor Lindsay went out of office, Rockefeller died, and so did the project. The south end of Staten Island has been nibbled by random development over the last thirty-five years. Much of it is still vacant. However, the financial planning craftsmanship in the report is still of value for future major urban developments.

Mayor John V. Lindsay
City of New York
City Hall
New York, New York 10001

May 1, 1970

Dear Mayor Lindsay:

The Rouse Company and its subsidiary, The American City Corporation, are pleased to submit this report concerning future development alternatives for South Richmond.

With the sensitive support of many City officials, this study was performed in an atmosphere which permitted us the freedom of seeking the best that might be, for the people of both Staten Island and the City of New York, on this extraordinary land resource.

From the inception of the study, we attempted to achieve a level of research, analysis, study and synthesis sufficient to permit incisive and rational conclusions. This report is not a plan, but rather a series of proposals of what might be in South Richmond. The many aspects of the urban scene have been analyzed and tested simultaneously. The relationship of housing, employment, environment, legal aspects, political realities, social considerations, and economic feasibility has been tested and balanced in an attempt to develop a spectrum of rational development programs for South Richmond. We engaged a broad range of specialists to assist with this study in order to assure a comprehensive inter-disciplinary approach. The role of the private sector was carefully defined and related to the necessary public involvement. What emerged is a firm conviction that here is a unique opportunity for that precise mixture of public purpose and private participation.

We believe that in South Richmond there is an unparalleled opportunity to conceive, design and bring into being a better place for people to grow, to live, to work and to play. It is an opportunity to create a "New City in the City"' where the quality of life for those who now live in South Richmond and for those who will come to live there, can be elevated to a level which will match their highest expectations. Moreover, such a New City can be enormously profitable to the City of New York and the people of Staten Island in several ways. A New City in South Richmond presents an opportunity to add substantial amounts of housing to the City's existing stock. A New City in South Richmond is capable of saving thousands of jobs that might normally leave the City and, indeed, it might dramatically reverse the current trend and result in thousands of new jobs coming to New York City. A New City undertaking could create a new prosperity for Staten Island with close to 10,000 construction jobs annually during the two decades of development. It would result in private sector investment of over $5 billion and an annual payroll, upon completion, in excess of $2 billion. Finally, and perhaps most importantly in this time of fiscal crisis for most cities, a New City in South Richmond can yield the City of New York over a billion dollars in revenue during the balance of the century above its financial investment in a New City undertaking.

Here, we earnestly believe, is an opportunity to create a New City which meets the goals of the City of New York and responds to the aspirations and hopes of the people of Staten Island. It is an opportunity to develop a direct relationship between housing and jobs while, at the same time, providing the broadest range of housing by type, tenure and cost. A New City in South Richmond can be accomplished within a time frame that we can all hope to see and, if undertaken with the spirit and enthusiasm that characterizes New York City, it is likely to meet the test of political acceptability. A New City in South Richmond is the most efficient and responsible way in which to respond to the growth that will occur under any circumstances. It is an opportunity to order that growth and to create a showplace both for the City of New York and the nation.

We believe there can be great support for the undertaking of a "New City in the City" in South Richmond. We stand ready to help in any way we can to further the cause of this important task.

Sincerely,

James W. Rouse

A REPORT TO THE CITY OF NEW YORK

John V. Lindsay, Mayor

An Analysis of Development Trends

and

Projections and Recommendations for a New City

in

South Richmond

Robert T. Connor, President

Borough of Richmond

The Rouse Company

May 1970

Excerpts from

"IT CAN HAPPEN HERE"

A Talk on Metropolitan Growth

by JAMES W. ROUSE

"We can't plan effectively for the future growth of American communities unless we start at the beginning—and that beginning is people."

"How can we really talk about what size a community should be, the structure of the community and its neighborhoods, whether or not it should be separated from another by greenbelts and open spaces, about big concentrated cities versus a collection of small towns around a center, until we have first asked and answered a lot of questions about what we are really trying to achieve in the community—what will contribute to the growth of people."

"I believe that the ultimate test of civilization is whether or not it contributes to the growth—improvement of mankind. Does it uplift, inspire, stimulate, and develop the best in man? There really can be no other right purpose of community except to provide an environment and an opportunity to develop better people. The most successful community would be that which contributed the most by its physical form, its institutions, and its operation to the growth of people."

"An inspired and concerned society will dignify man; will find ways to develop his talents; will put the fruits of his labor and intellect to effective use; will struggle for brotherhood and for the elimination of bigotry and intolerance; will care for the indigent, the delinquent, the sick, the aged; will seek the truth and communicate it; will respect differences among men. The raising of such a target would provide direction and purpose and basic testing for the pieces of planning which ultimately make the whole community. To shoot at it all would require questions and answers that aren't flowing today among the people planning and developing our communities."

"Personally, I hold some very unscientific conclusions to the effect that people grow best in small communities where the institutions which are the dominant forces in their lives are within the scale of their comprehension and within reach of their sense of responsibility and capacity to manage. I believe that a broader range of friendships and relationships occurs in a village or small town than in a city; that self-reliance is promoted; that relationship to nature—to the out-of-doors—to the freer forms of recreation and human activity is encouraged in a smaller community."

"I believe there should be a strong infusion of nature—natural nature—not sterilized and contrived nature—throughout a network of towns; that people should be able to fish and watch birds; find solitude; study nature in a natural environment; feel the spaces of nature—all as a part of his everyday life."

"What are we waiting for? I'll tell you what—for plans and proposals big enough to solve our problems. People are drawn by logic and reason and by a deep yearning for order, beauty, and a good life to the plans that deal with real problems and offer real solutions. They will rise to the big and dramatically good plans—they will yawn at the timid, the cautious, the unconvincing."

"Here then is the challenge of The Good Environment—not a call to raise huge new funds; nor to marshal new pools of manpower. It is simply to change our attitudes towards our community."

"To harness these new attitudes to the forces already in motion and to the resources that already exist among us will generate a new, creative thrust that will not only produce new communities but will release among the people in them the potential for the noblest civilization the world has ever known."

On September 26, 1963, Mr. James W. Rouse, President of The Rouse Company, speaking at a University of California Conference on "The Metropolitan Future," said some things that are as valid today as they were then.

The principles espoused by Mr. Rouse over six years ago and indeed the title of his talk "It Can Happen Here" are, in fact, the heart of this report to the City of New York and the people of Staten Island. The conclusions and recommendations of this report carry that theme forward.

v

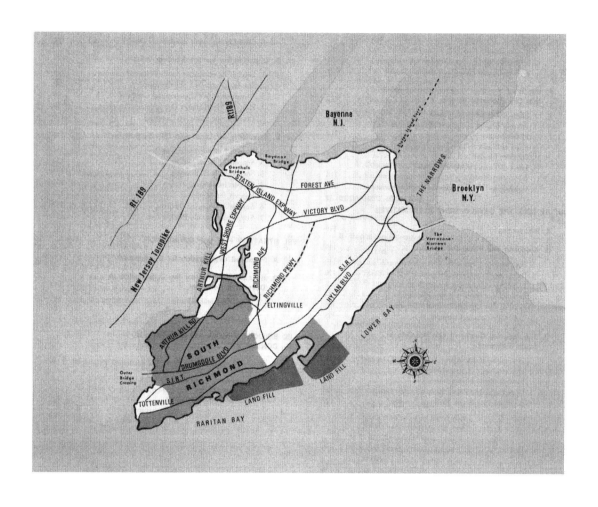

A. Introduction

In this section, the economic implications of the trend and New City development programs are compared. First, the economic measures are described. These measures provide the basis for economic comparisons between the development programs. They involve questions of private development economics as well as municipal finance. The second part of this section presents a brief description of the methodology used to formulate and compare the economic consequences of the alternative development programs. This is followed by a summary of the major inputs used in the modeling process. The final two parts of this section set forth the economic models for the basic alternative development programs and estimate the economic consequences of the variables introduced in the previous section. They are:

1. The introduction of a tunnel into the trend model,

2. The absence of a tunnel in the high-density New City model,

3. The reduction of land area for the New City models by assuming no off-shore landfill and,

4. The application to the New City models of a housing profile that would allot 70% of the units to low-income and middle-income families.

B. Economic Measures

Five basic measures are used to compare the trend development program and a New City in South Richmond and to compare the New City models one to another.

• Return to the City, considering its land as a liquid asset that can either be liquidated in the trend development of South Richmond or in the context of a New City.

• Economic feasibility of the land development entailed by a commitment to build a New City in South Richmond.

• Feasibility of providing the special community facilities and services envisioned for a New City.

• The effects of trend and New City development on City capital expenditures, both within and outside the debt ceiling.

• Net revenue flows to the City, expressed in hypothetical terms as an expense budget for South Richmond, given trend development or a commitment to a New City. (Net revenues are the difference between taxes and other revenues that would be derived from South Richmond, and the cost of providing municipal facilities and services.)

a) Total Net Revenue Flow at Full Development

The annual net revenue flows to the City of New York after full development of the study area would be significantly higher with New City development in South Richmond. The difference between the middle-density New City model, for example, and the trend model—in the analysis presented in the previous section—was $83.2 million annually, with New City revenue over 100% higher than the trend net revenue figure.

Table VII-B1
Net Revenue Flows for All Models at Full Development

Development Models	Dwelling Units Added	Assessable Base	Annual Net Revenues at Full Development	Per Dwelling Net Revenues at Full Development
		(in $ millions)	(in $ millions)	($)
Trend	70,000	2,334.6	55.6	791
New City				
Low-Density	94,000	3,549.1	97.6	1,038
Middle-Density	150,000	5,372.7	137.6	917
High-Density	250,000	9,111.0	219.5	878

b) Per Unit Net Revenue at Full Development

Taking population into account, Table VII-B1 shows that per dwelling net revenue flows would also be higher for New City than for trend development in South Richmond.

In comparing the trend and New City per unit figures, it is important to recall that a significant number of units in all the New City models involved tax abatements. If, for example, the per dwelling figures were derived for the New City models before tax abatements they would be as follows:

Low-Density Model	$1,135 per dwelling
Middle-Density Model	$1,160 per dwelling
High-Density Model	$1,317 per dwelling

The effect of tax abatements on comparative net revenue analysis was indicated in Table VI-E2, in the previous section, which compared real estate tax potential for the New City models with real estate taxes after tax abatements for each model. It is very apparent that high-density development is most affected by low-income and middle-income housing. This is because a greater proportion of housing units would have to receive tax abatements in a New City where mid-rise and high-rise apartment buildings, with their higher construction costs, make up a greater segment of the housing to be offered. The discussion of low-income and middle-income housing in the previous section indicates that a low-density New City, on the other hand, would offer the most efficient way to meet a housing profile where 55% or 70% of the residents were to be low-income and middle-income families.

c) Present Value of Cumulative Net Revenue Flows, 1970-2005

The third significant comparison that can be made concerning net revenue flows to the City from alternative development courses in South Richmond, is between the present value of those flows over a sufficiently long period of time. The following table indicates the absolute and present value of net flows to the City over the 35-year period for the basic models considered in the previous section.

Table VII-B2
Present Value of Net Revenue Flows to City Through 2005—All Models

Development Model	Cumulative Net Revenues 1970-2005	Year in Which Full Development Reached	Present Value[1] of Cumulative Net Revenues 1970-2005
	(in $ millions)		(in $ millions)
Trend	744.4	2005	173.0
New City			
Low-Density	2,093.6	1988	574.0
Middle-Density	2,723.4	1992	689.7
High-Density	2,378.9	2005	509.6

[1] Computed at 6% discount rate.

The potential gains to the City from undertaking a New City in South Richmond are dramatic. Because of pace of development combined with scale, the middle-density model would produce the greatest cumulative gains to the City over the next 35 years.

2. Land Development Feasibility

It is believed that the land development process, necessary to produce a New City in South Richmond, is economically viable. Three factors, however, differentiate the three representative New City models from each other:

• The level of profit, measured in terms of present value,

• The City commitment required to produce acceptable financing ratios, measured in terms of payment for its land, and taxes or in-lieu payments on undeveloped land, and

• The amount of time it takes to begin to produce a profit from the land development process.

a) Present Value of Land Development Profits Compared

It is believed that the highest level of profits, measured in terms of their present value, could be derived from low-density New City development. The summary tables indicated the following figures:

Table VII-B3
Present Value of Land Development Profits for Alternative New City Models
(in $ millions)

New City Models	Total Net Position At End of Development (Profit)	Present Value[1] of Land Development (Profit)
Low-Density	182.2	67.7
Middle-Density	193.3	56.9
High-Density	393.3	57.5

[1] Computed at 6% discount rate.

The profit potentials indicated above require significantly different levels of investment or commitment by the City in terms of their land and real estate taxes on undeveloped land paid by the development entity through the

South Richmond's vacant land presents a rare opportunity.

life of the project. The most significant measure will come later, when land development profits are considered in the context of required investment or opportunity costs which take into account land development tax abatements. Two points, however, are relevant in considering the figures in Table VII-B3:

• First, a New City characterized by low-density development, even while having the lowest total returns, benefits in terms of present value land development economics from its rapid pace of development over a relatively short period. To repeat, pace is achieved because of the scarcity of the predominant type of housing—single-family and two-family detached homes—in close proximity to Manhattan. The development period is short because low-density development most rapidly consumes the New City land resource.

• At the other end of the spectrum, high-density development could be expected to achieve the highest net returns in absolute terms, but the returns are realized so far into the development period that their present value is significantly reduced.

b) City Commitment Compared

Although it produces the lowest returns in terms of present value, the middle-density model would require the least financial sacrifice by the City in the land development process. As noted in Section VI, the middle-density New City development in South Richmond would be able to produce an acceptable financing ratio without requiring the City to forego either early payments for its land or taxes on undeveloped land held by the development entity. For the low-density and high-density New City programs, on the other hand, it had to be assumed in the economic models that the City would delay or forego at least one and sometimes both of these potential proceeds.

When a tunnel was eliminated from the high-density development program, the land area reduced, or a higher proportion of low-income and middle-

income housing specified, the City commitment necessary to produce acceptable financing ratios had to expand. The relationships between the models, in terms of present value of returns, however, remained the same—middle-density most favorable, low-density next, and high-density New City development least favorable.

The significance of the level of sacrifice, or investment that the City would have to make to achieve an acceptable financing ratio is considered when total returns to the City are compared.

Table VII-B4

Commitment of City Land and/or Taxes on Undeveloped Land
Required to Produce Acceptable Financing Ratios

New City Models and Variations	Payment for City-Owned Land	In Lieu Payments Taxes to City on Undeveloped Land
Low-Density		
Basic Model	No	Yes
Without Off-Shore Land	No	No
With 70% Low-Income and Middle-Income Housing	No	No
Middle-Density		
Basic Model	Yes	Yes
Without Off-Shore Land	No	No
With 70% Low-Income and Middle-Income Housing	Yes	No
High-Density		
Basic Model	No	Yes, but only ¼
Without Off-Shore Land	No	No
With 70% Low-Income and Middle-Income Housing	No	No

c) Number of Years to Start of Profits Compared

Because of its shorter development period, the low-density New City model produced the shortest turn-around period (the period of time after land assembly and development begins before the venture begins to show positive cumulative cash flows). The middle-density New City takes slightly longer, and the high-density model the longest.

Another important consideration, related to both peak debt and the turn-around period, is the period of time after land assembly and development begins that it takes to begin to generate positive cash flows. This is, in effect, the year of peak debt. The relationship between the start of land disposition, 1975, and the beginning of positive annual cash flows is shown below for the three New City models.

Table VII-B5

Years from Start of Land Disposition to Peak Debt and
Start of Profits for New City Models

New City Models	Years from Start of Land Disposition to		
	Full Development	Peak Debt	Start of Profits
Low-Density	13 (1975-1988)	3 (1978)	11 (1986)
Middle-Density	17 (1975-1992)	4 (1979)	15 (1990)
High-Density	30 (1975-2005)	14 (1989)	25 (2000)

In all of the models, it is not until very late in the development that profits begin, even though positive cash flows begin much earlier. This is because of the extremely high debt that is generated almost immediately by having to acquire over $240 million of land in the first five years of the project. The consequence, as related to financing, of carrying land for long periods, is taken into account through the financing ratio.

3. Feasibility of Providing Special Community Facilities and Services

The economic models in the previous section show that the special community facilities and services needed to create the values and pace for a New City in South Richmond can be financed through a special assessment. The special assessment would be levied by a separate New City entity without any burden or required involvement on the part of New York City. The relationship between this special assessment and property values is shown below. The total and per dwelling special capital and operating costs for the three New City models that produce the assessment are repeated below. Once again, the efficiencies of scale are evident.

Table VII-B6

Special Assessment and Total and Per Dwelling Unit Special Capital and Operating Costs for New City Models at Full Development

New City Model	Total Dwelling Units	Capital Costs		Operating Costs		Approximate Assessment per $100 Assessed Value
		Total	Per Dwelling Unit	Total	Per Dwelling Unit	
		($ millions)	($)	($ millions)	($)	($)
Low-Density	94,000	$139.0	$1,480	$13.0	$140	0.90
Middle-Density	150,000	168.6	1,125	18.8	125	0.90
High-Density	250,000	219.8	880	26.0	105	0.90

The special assessment in a South Richmond New City would approximate a 20% surcharge on the existing New York City real estate taxes for property owners in the project area. This level of special assessment, less than 10% of normal residential shelter budgets and less than 5% of commercial rents, would not be expected to affect residential, business or industrial market support for a New City in South Richmond adversely. Experience in the several large-scale community development projects in the United States indicates, beyond any question, that people, businesses and industry are willing to pay more for a special environment. In the new city of Columbia, Maryland, for example, a 20% surcharge on the normal Howard County tax rate is levied for special facilities and services without an adverse effect on market support. In fact, in most large-scale new community projects, the special community facilities and services that are being provided are essential to the new city's success in attracting business and industry as well as new families. In the New York area, where a lack of many community amenities and conveniences has come to be a part of life, the potential market impact of the special facilities and services envisioned for a New City in South Richmond should be enormous.

4. Level of City Capital Investment Required

In the previous section, several important factors regarding City investment in South Richmond were considered:

- Total level of City investment required,
- The amount of public investment that would be within the debt ceiling,
- Investment efficiency, or capital costs per dwelling, and
- The average annual level of investment required.

a) Total Level of City Investment Compared

Because of major uncertainties regarding the City's responsibility for street and sewer costs, given the current outlook, it is extremely difficult to compare the total levels of public investment required of the City in South Richmond for trend versus New City development. The New City models anticipate the land development entity meeting all costs for streets, sewers and drainage. The trend economic model was based on private developers installing 60% of all streets, drainage, and sewers in South Richmond. It could be argued, however, that inadequate construction, particularly in the case of streets will, over time, result in the City making nearly the full investment in streets and sewers in South Richmond.

Table VII-B7 shows the total investment that might be required of the City for each of the South Richmond development alternatives, with two different figures cited for trend development; one indicating the full investment in infrastructure, and the other, the 40% figure used in the economic models, to represent City capital costs for streets, sewers and drainage during the development period.

Table VII-B7

Capital Costs to the City for Trend and New City Development

Alternative Development Models	Dwelling Units	Standard Municipal Account Costs	
		Total ($ millions)	Per Unit ($)
Trend Development	70,000		
City Pays:			
40% Sewer, Drainage, Road Costs		322.1	4,600
100% Sewer, Drainage, Road Costs		431.8	6,168
New City Models			
Low-Density	94,000	425.8	4,526
Middle-Density	150,000	528.6	3,524
High-Density	250,000	681.7	2,727

b) City Capital Investment Per Capita Compared

Even with the private sector assuming 60% of street and sewer costs under trend development, Table VII-B7 shows that the lowest per dwelling unit capital outlays required of the City for future development in South Richmond would come with New City development. The table also shows that if the City ultimately has to make the full investment in streets, drainage, and sewers in South Richmond, the difference is far more dramatic. The lower per capita investment required of the City in the New City models is possible primarily because all street, drainage, and sewer costs would be borne by the land development entity, with the exception of major highways and the interceptor sewer system at the level currently planned. It should be remembered that improvements to the interceptor sewer system for the New City models greater than currently planned were assumed to be the responsibility of the land development entity.

In comparing the New City models, the figures in Table VII-B8 imply that low-density development in South Richmond would represent an underutilization of certain major improvements that will be made; for example, the interceptor sewer. High-density development, on the other hand, clearly achieves efficiencies of scale.

Table VII-B8

Comparison of Standard Municipal Capital Costs Within and Outside the City Debt Limit for Trend and New City Development

Alternative Development Models	Standard Municipal Capital Costs (in $ millions)		
	Total Amount	Amount Within Limit	Amount Outside Limit
Trend Development			
w/40% Sewer, Drainage, Road Costs	$322.1	213.5	108.6
w/100% Sewer, Drainage, Road Costs	431.8	250.6	181.2
New City Development			
Low-Density	425.8	310.5	115.3
Middle-Density	528.6	408.2	120.4
High-Density	681.7	559.8	121.9

The figures in Table VII-B8 reflect the assumption used in the economic models that two-thirds of the costs of public transit improvements would be met by State or Federal grants. If the City had to incur the total cost projected for ferry, SIRT, and in the case of high-density New City development, tunnel improvements, capital costs would be somewhat greater. As shown below, the most substantial increase would be in the high-density New City municipal account, because of the tunnel.

Table VII-B9

Municipal Account Capital Costs Increases Without Two-thirds Grant for Public Transit Improvements

(in $ millions)

Alternative Development Models	Increases in Capital Costs	Average Annual Investment Required with Increase
Trend Development		
40% Sewer, Drainage, Road Costs	25.2	10.1
100% Sewer, Drainage, Road Costs	25.2	10.5
New City Development		
Low-Density	53.4	36.8
Middle-Density	65.1	34.9
High-Density	231.1	30.4

The increases cited above would be totally within the debt limit.

c) Capital Investment Within and Outside the Debt Limit Compared

Perhaps more significant than total per unit capital investment required by the City, is the amount of investment that would be considered within the City's legal debt limit. The figures in Table VII-B8 show that according to the economic models, the New City development programs would require substantial increases in spending within the debt ceiling, greater in proportion than the total increase in capital costs between trend and New City development.

d) Average Levels of City Investment Compared

New City development in South Richmond would clearly require a change in priority regarding City capital investment in Staten Island. Not only would the total capital investment and investment inside the debt ceiling be greater if a new city were developed in South Richmond, but the average annual rate of spending in Staten Island would, as shown below, have to be substantially increased.

Table VII-B10

Average Annual Capital Expenditures for Trend and New City Development

Reference Figures

Alternative Development Models	Dwelling Units	Total Capital Costs	Development Period	Average Annual Investment Required
		($ millions)	(years)	($ millions)
Trend Development	70,000		35	
City pays:				
40% Sewer, Drainage, Road Costs		322.1		9.2
100% Sewer, Drainage, Road Costs		431.8		12.3
New City Development				
Low-Density	94,000	425.8	13	32.7
Middle-Density	150,000	528.6	17	31.1
High-Density	250,000	681.7	30	22.7

5. Total City Returns Compared

The concept of relating the various returns to the City, possible from South Richmond, to its total investment was set forth in the previous section. The returns and costs (or investments) that were considered are as follows:

Investments
- City-owned land
- Capital costs—sewer, water, streets, schools, etc.
- Taxes abated

Returns
- Net revenue flows
- Proceeds from sale of City land
- Land development profits

Two meaningful combinations of these costs and returns were identified:

Return on City-owned land, related in trend development to its sale on the open market; and, in New City development, to the total proceeds from the sale of the land to a land development entity and the profits from land development.

Return on City capital investment in public facilities and services as related to ongoing net revenue flows.

IX
BIBLIOGRAPHICAL REFERENCES AND CONSULTANTS

A. Study Participants

For the City of New York:
The South Richmond Development Policy Committee

DONALD ELLIOTT...........................Chairman, City Planning Commission
DAVID A. GROSSMAN.......................Deputy Director, Bureau of the Budget
ROBERT G. HAZEN.........................Commissioner of Development, Housing and Development Administration
AUGUST HECKSCHER......................Administrator, Parks, Recreation and Cultural Affairs Administration
HOLT MEYER..............................Director, Office of Staten Island Development, and Chairman, South Richmond Development Policy Committee
CONSTANTINE SIDAMON-ERISTOFF............Administrator, Transportation Administration
MATHIAS L. SPIEGEL.......................Formerly First Deputy Administrator, Environmental Protection Administration

The Rouse Company/American City Corporation:
South Richmond Planning Study Policy Board

JAMES W. ROUSE..........................President, The Rouse Company
WILLIAM E. FINLEY.......................Vice President, The Rouse Company
LEO MOLINARO............................President, The American City Corporation
MORTON HOPPENFELD......................Vice President, The Rouse Company
RICHARD L. ANDERSON......................Vice President, The Rouse Company

South Richmond Planning Study Staff

WILLIAM E. FINLEY.......................Project Director
ED AUERBACH.............................Project Coordinator
RICHARD P. BROWNE.......................Project Engineer
JAMES T. BUCK..........................Financial Analyst
MATHIAS J. DEVITO.......................Senior Vice President and General Counsel, The Rouse Company
FRANK GENZER............................Project Planner
WALLACE HAMILTON.......................Director of Institutional Planning
ROBERT W. MOSS.........................Project Planner
MARC OLDER.............................Project Planner
JAMES E. SMITH, JR. ....Financial Analyst
MICHAEL D. SPEAR........................Director of Research and Project Evaluation

139

POSTSCRIPT

This book is but a small first step toward creating a movement aimed at CURING URBANITIS. Although it's akin to turning around a battleship that is using its nuclear power to plow over the horizon, the power of the right idea or interlocking cluster of ideas can send a message to the captain to slow down and turn to a new direction.

Fortunately or unfortunately, the ship of uncontrolled urban growth has no single captain. It has thousands of leaders, each with his or her own agenda, attitudes, and comfort level. To get them to stand up taller and see what direction their ships are going and to listen to the benefits of changing directions and methods of development is not an easy task.

If the notions presented here are heard and only a few captains take note, the turning will have started. The success of this effort will be measured in decades, maybe generations. Considering how long the ship of urban decay and sprawl has been cruising along, that schedule could be acceptable.

The U.S. population grew from 200 to 300 million in just forty years. The demographers have gone out on a limb and projected that the number will be 600 million by the beginning of the next century. Imagine our larger metropolitan cities becoming like Mexico City or Sao Paulo, now both over twenty-five million. The time to sound the alarm is now.

There are two sequels to this book now being planned. The first will be a detailed description of the upcoming exploration to find sites for the first few new "MetroCities" of 500,000 each, as described in Chapters 7 and 9. Teams will be sent into the areas indicated on the map showing potential sites and a full range of preliminary studies will lead to an understanding of the promises and pitfalls of each location. The process will reveal a deep understanding of the feasibility of building such massive developments over the coming decades.

The third book will portray ideas and concepts of winners of a national urban planning and design competition held to glean the most advanced ideas for the structure, functions, and components for a model "MetroCity" for 500,000 people on 64,000 acres.

The competitors will be given a theoretical site containing an array of realistic limitations, physical barriers, systems requirements, access and development conditions, leading to a pollution-free environment. The competitors will be called upon to deal with advanced requirements on matters of education, natural resources, sustainability, housing innovations, transportation systems, staged development, and financial constraints. The competition will be held under the auspices of a non-profit corporation with experience in urban affairs.

The author welcomes comments and suggestions on how to foster support for the concepts of urban change covered in this book.

William E. Finley

picb@gate.net

Bibliography for *Curing Urbanitis*

American Planning Association, *The Principles of Smart Development*, PAS Report 479, Chicago 1998

Barnett, Jonathon, *Planning for a New Century-The Regional Agenda*
Island Press 2001

_____, *The Fractured Metropolis*, Harper Collins 1995

Benfield, F. Kaid, *Solving Sprawl: Models of Smart Growth in Communities Across America*, National Research Defense Council 2001

Bloom, Nicholas D, *Suburban Alchemy*, Ohio State University press 2001

Bolton, Arthur, *A Strategy for Distressed Neighborhoods*, Western Consortium for Public Health 1994

Branch, Melville C, *Comprehensive Planning for the 21st Century: General Theory and Principles*, Westport CT: Praeger 1998

Breckenfeld, Gurney, *Columbia and the New Cities*, NY Ives Washburn 1971

Brown, Lester R, *PLAN B 2.0: Repairing a Planet Under Stress and a Civilization in Trouble*, NY Norton 2006

Bruegmann, Robert, *Sprawl: A Compact History*, University of Chicago Press 2005

Burschell, Robert, *The Costs of Sprawl – Revisited*, Transportation Research Board 1998

Burkhart, Lynne, *Old Values in a New Town: The Politics of Race and Class in Columbia, MD*, NY Praeger, 1981

Cervero, Robert, *The Transit Metropolis: A Global Inquiry*, Washington D, Island Press 1998

Calethorp, Peter, *The Next American Metropolis*, Princeton Architectural Press 1993

Census 2000, *Statistical Abstract*, Washington DC, GPO 2002

Chapin, Tim and Charles Connerly, Harrison Higgins, *Growth Management in Florida: Planning for Paradise*, Ashgate Publishing, Burlington VT 2007

Charles, J.A., *Lessons from the Portland Experience*, Heritage Foundation 2000

Committee for Economic Development, Research & Policies: *A New Approach to the Nation's Urban Crisis* NY 1995

Cosby, Bill and Alvin F. Poussaint, MD, *Come On, People*, Thomas Nelson Nashville 2007

Costigan, Patrick, *A Comprehensive Approach to Rebuilding Poor Neighborhoods*, Georgia Academy Journal, 1999

Chaskin, Robert and Prudence Brown, *Theories of Neighborhood Change*,Chicago: Chapin Hall Center for Children 1996

Chudacoff, Howard, *Major Problems in American Urban History* NY Heath 1993

Dietrich, W., *How Progress Ate America*, American Forests 1999

Duany, Andres and Elizabeth Plater-Zyberk, *The Rise of Sprawl and the Decline of the American Dream*, NY North Point Press 2000

Dunphy, Robert T., *Moving Beyond Gridlock*, Urban Land Institute 1997

Eichler, Edward and Marshall Kaplan, *The Community Builders*, Berkeley: University of California Press 1967

Faludi, Andreas, *European Spatial Planning*, Toronto, Lincoln Institute of Land Policy 2002

Finley, William E., *Boomer Times & Senior Life: Living the New Millennium: The Future of American Cities*

February 2007
_____: *A Noble Step To Stopping Sprawl..British New Towns*
March 2007
_____: *New Towns for America..Too Little and Too Late*
April 2007
_____: *What's So Special About Portland?*
May 2007
_____: *When Did We Lose the War on Poverty?*
July 2007
_____: *A Glimpse into the Future: A MegaCity in Holland?*
August 2007
_____: *Is Florida Planning for the Hispanic Invasion?*
October 2007
_____: *Atlanta's Going Dry? It's the Population, Stupid!*
November 2007
_____: *A Floridian's View of Climate Change*
January 2008
_____: *An Automotive Revolution: The Good and the Bad*

February 2008

Fodor, Eben, *Better Not Bigger*, New Society Publishers 1999

Forsythe, Ann, *ReFormInG Suburbia*, Berkeley: University of California Press 2005

Fulton, William, *The Reluctant Metropolis: The Politics of Urban Growth in Los Angeles*, Solano Press Books 1997

Gardner, John, *Community Planning: An Overview Report & Case Profiles*, Washington DC, Teamworks 1993

Garvin, Alexander, *The American City: What Works, What Doesn't*, NY McGraw Hill 1996

Gordon, Peter and Harry Richardson, *Are Compact Cities A Desirable Planning Goal?* American Planning Association Journal, Winter 1997

Gottlieb, Robert, *Reinventing Los Angeles*, The MIT Press 2007

Gottman, J., *Megalopolis*, Cambridge: The MIT Press 1961

Harvey, F. Barton, *Community Rebuilding: A Quiet Revolution*, National Civic Review 1996

Hall, Dee, *The Choice: High Density or Urban Sprawl: Portland Gets Creative*, Wisconsin State journal, 1995

Hall, Peter, *Cities of Tomorrow: An intellectual History of Urban Planning in the 20th Century*, Oxford, Blackwell 1996

Haydon, Dolores, *A Field Guide to Sprawl*, NY, W.W. Norton & Co. 2004

Hirschhorn, Joel S., *Sprawl Kills*, NY Sterling & Ross 2005

Hoppenfeld, Morton, *A Sketch of the Planning and Building Process for Columbia, MD*, APA Journal November 1967

Institute of Portland Metropolitan Studies, *A Pathway to Sustainability*, Portland OR 1995

Jacobs, Jane, *The Death and Life of American Cities*, NY: Random House 1961

_____, *Dark Age Ahead*, Vantage Books 2005

Johnson, Elmer W., *Avoiding the Collision of Cities and Cars*, American Academy of Arts & Sciences, Chicago 1993

Katz, Bruce and Jennifer Johnson, Karen Brown, Mary Cunningham and Noah Sawyer, *Rethinking Local Affordable Housing Strategies*, DC: Brookings Inst. 2003

Kelbaugh, Douglas S., *Repairing the American Metropolis*, Seattle; Univ. of Washington Press 2002

Kingsley, G. Thomas and Martin Ahravanel, Mary Cunningham, Jeremy Gustavson, Arthur Naparstek and Margery Turner, *Lessons for the Future of Public Housing*, DC Urban Institute 2003

Langdon, Philip, *A Better Place to Live: Reshaping the American Suburb,* Cambridge: Univ. of Mass. Press 1994

Leinberger, Christopher B., *The Option of Urbanism*, Island Press 2008

Lucy, William and David L. Phillips, *Tomorrow's Cities, Tomorrow's Suburbs*, American Planning Association 2006

Mansfield, Todd and Ross and L. Beth Yockey, *Craving Community: The New American Dream*, Seattle: Yockey Communications 2007

Minkler, Meredith, *Community Organizing Among Low Income Elderly,* New Brunswick NJ: Rutgers Univ. Press 1997

Mitchell, Joseph and David L. Stebenne, *New City On A Hill*: *A History of Columbia MD,* Charleston SC: The History Press 2007

Mumford, Lewis, *In the Name of Sanity*, Harcourt Brace & Co. 1954

Munzer, Martha and John Vogel, Jr., *New Towns: Building Cities from Scratch*, NT Alfred A. Knopf 1974

Myers-Lipton, Scott J., Social *Solutions to Poverty*, Boulder CO, Paradigm Publishers 2006

Olsen, Joshua, *Better Places, Better Lives: A Biography of James W. Rouse,* DC, ULI 2003

Orfield, Myron, *Metropolitics*, DC Brookings 1997

Pierce, Neal and Carol Sternbach, *Enterprise Communities: Community-based Development in America*, DC 1990

_____, Planetizen *Contemporary Debates in Urban Planning*, DC Island Press 2007

Porter, Douglas R., *A 50 Year Plan for Metropolitan Portland*, DC: ULI 1995

_____, *Managing Growth in American Communities*, DC Island Press 2008

Puentes, Robert and David Warren, *One Fifth of America: A Comprehensive Guide to America's First Suburbs*, DC Brookings 2006

Real Estate Research Corporation, *The Costs of Sprawl*, Sierra Club 1974

Rusk, David, *Baltimore Unbound: A Strategy for Regional Renewal*, Baltimore: The Abell Foundation 1996

_____, *Cities Without Suburbs*, DC Woodrow Wilson Center Press 1993

_____, *Inside Game, Outside Game*, DC Brookings 1999

Rutherford, H. Platt, *The Human Metropolis*, Univ of Mass. & Lincoln Inst. Of Land Policies 2006

Rykwert, Joseph, *Seduction of Place: The City in the 20th Century and Beyond*, NY Pantheon Books 2000

Schwartz, Peter, *The Art of the Long View: Planning for the Future in an Uncertain World*, NY Doubleday 1996

Sitte, Camilo, *The Art of Building Cities*, Westport CT Hyperion Press 1979

Tennenbaum, Robert, Editor: *Creating the New City: Columbia MD* Perry Publishing and the Partners in Community Building 1996

Weiss, Shirley, *New Town Development in the United States; Experiments in Private Entrepreneurship*, Chapel Hill, Univ. of North Carolina Press 1973

Wells, Malcolm, *Recovering America: A more Gentle Way to Build*, Cape Cod MA 1990

Yaro, Robert and Tony Hiss, *A Region at Risk: The 3rd Regional Plan for the NY, NJ, CT Metropolitan Area*, DC Island Press 1996

INDEX

Adirondack Park   130
Almere, new town in
    Netherlands   123
America is a Metropolitan
    Nation – Brookings Inst   22
American City Corporation,
    consulting arm of The
    Rouse Co. 167
American Dream   23
American new towns   108
American Samoa   5
Arena at Clematis, West Palm
    Beach FL   6

Baby Boom Generation   25
Bain, Henry   117
Baltimore – experiments in
    inner-city renewal   43
Bartholomew, Harland   15
Biking in big cities   145
Bloomberg, Michael, Mayor of
    New York City   35
Borut, Alan   15
British Eco-towns   122
British new town development
    corporations   103
British new town program
    104
Brooks, David, *New York Times,*
    July 2007 on Holistic
    Change   134
Browne, Richard, The
    Woodlands TX   15, 109
Bulgaria, USAID Seminars   7
Bush, George W.   29

Calethorpe, Peter, California
    architect-planner   86
Canada, Geoffrey, Harlem
    Project   46
Carbonell, Armando, New York
    Regional Plan Assoc.   128
Cedar-Riverside New-town-in-
    town, Minneapolis MN   6,
    110
Chayes, Antonia, Columbia
    Work Group   118
Chicago 1933 World's Fair   32
China, Urban Growth
    Policies   87
Columbia MD Goals   117
Columbia MD Land Use
    Formulae   77
Columbia MD, Howard County
    School System   120
Cost/Benefit Studies   29
Council of Governments   31
Corbett, John, President/CEO
    Palm Beach Housing
    Partnership   15
Crawford, Robert, Recreation
    Consultant, Columbia Work
    Group   117
Connecticut General Life
    Insurance Co   110
Creating the New City, Edited
    by Robert Tennenbaum   7

Dade County (now Miami-Dade
    County) Urban Growth
    Boundary   62

Delray Beach Redevelopment
Agency 6

East Baltimore, JohnsHopkins
Redevelopment Project
45
Edwards, John, candidate for
President, on Poverty 59
Eisenhower, Dwight, President,
Nat. Defense Highway
System 28
Enterprise Foundation 44
Environmental Impact Studies
for new MetroCities 126
Environmental Protection
Agency, founded in
1969 95
Euclid, OH, first Zoning
Ordinance. 28

Faludi, Andrea, author
of European Spatial
Planning 127
FEMA sponsored rebuilding of
Princeville, NC 7
Finley, Anita 15, 17
Finley, William recruited by
James Rouse, 1962 111,
147
____ Background Statement 5
Foote, Nelson of General
Electric, Columbia Work
Group 116
Ford Motors goes Green 69
Forsythe, Ann - author of
Reforming Suburbia 108

Gans, Herbert PhD, Urban
Sociologist, Columbia Work
Group 118

Gehry, Frank, Architect,
Columbia Exhibit Bldg,
Marjory Merriwether
Post Pavilion of Music,
Rouse Company
Headquarters 119
Gladstone, Robert, Advisor
on urban economics and
Columbia financial
model, Work Group
Member 117
Google offers employee
transit 34
Gore, Al, Environmentalist 30
Graves, Richard, Director
California League of Cities,
candidate for
Governor 15
Green Cities – new MetroCities
to be green 79

Harlem Project – New York
City 46
Harvey, Bart CEO Enterprise
Foundation 45
Hirschorn, Joel PhD author
Sprawl Kills 31
Holistic Caring 42, 76
Homestead FL – Rebuilt after
Hurricane Andrew 6
Hong Kong 61
Hoppenfeld, Mort, Chief
Planner, Columbia MD 111
Horizon Corporation – Owner of
Waterwood TX 6
House, Carl – Economic
Modeler, Columbia MD 15
Housing Partnership 8
Humphrey, Hubert, Vice
President 119

HUD – US Dept of Housing and
    Urban Development   13, 95

Irvine Ranch CA 109
India – Urban Growth Policies   87
Immigration – US Policies   54
Inside Game, Outside Game by
    David Rusk   46
Indianapolis IN   30
"I, too, have a dream"   19
Inskoy New Town, Siberia, RF   6
Interama, North Miami FL   5

Jacksonville, FL 30
Jacobson, William   15
Jencks, Christopher, Harvard
    Education Expert,
    Columbia Work Group   117
JohnsHopkins Hospital   45
Johnson, Lyndon, President, on
    Poverty   58

Kennedy, John, President,
    on putting a man on the
    moon   93, 147
Kent, T.Jack, Chair, Dept of City
    and Regional Planning,
    University of California at
    Berkeley   15
King, Martin Luther, Jr, "I have a
    dream"   19

Lemkau, Paul Dr. JohnsHopkins
    University/Medical School,
    Expert on Health Care
    Systems, Columbia Work
    Group   117
Lindsay, John, Mayor, New York
    City, proposed new city
    on Staten Island   167

Live to be 100 PLUS by Anita
    and Bill Finley   7
Living the New Millennium by Bill
    Finley, in
    Boomer Times & Senior Life
    1999 to present   7
Local Development
    Corporations in new
    MetroCities   98
London, Heathrow Airport,
    new Personal Transport
    System   89
Los Angeles, City of Angels   48
____ Polluted beaches   57
Louisville KN   30

Masdar Institute, Abu
    Dhabi   140
Molinaro, Leo, President,
    American City Corporation,
    consulting arm of The
    Rouse Company   167
Mason, William, President, The
    Irvine Ranch   109
MacArthur Foundation   6
McHarg, Ian, Prof. Landscape
    Design, University of
    Pennsylvania,
    Consultant to The
    Woodlands   109
McNamara, Patrick, CEO,
    Community Partnership
    Group,
    Palm Beach County   15
Metropolitan Planning
    Organizations mandated
    by Federal
    Transportation planning
    regulations   29

Michaels, Donald, Harvard
    Social Psychologist, Chair,
    Columbia Work Group   117
Milton Keynes, British new
    city   107;
    new energy systems   123
"Minorities" now 1/3 of US
    population   56
Mitchell, George, Founder, The
    Woodlands TX   109

Mitchell, Robert   15
Montgomery County MD   41

National Capital Planning
    Commission   5
National Governors'
    Association   31
New Delhi   91
New US Urban Development
    Policies   133
National Partnership for
    MetroCities – A non-profit
    corporation
    In the public interest   94,
    128, 136
New MetroCities – Purpose in
    building them   75, 125
New MetroCities – Potential
    Locations   129
    1. North central
        Pennsylvania
    2. SW Georgia
    3. Near Lima, OH
    4. South central Illinois
    5. Near Abilene TX
    6. South central New
        Mexico
    7. Near Tonapah NV
    8. Near Needles CA

National Partnership Matching
    Funds   99
New South Richmond
    Report   167
New York City Public
    Housing   101
The Next America- Columbia
    MD Exhibit 1967   111
NIMBY Factor – Not in my
    backyard   28
National policies on urban
    growth   133, 135

O'Connell, Dan   15
Olsen, Josh, author Biography
    of James Rouse,
    Better Places, Better Lives   121
O'Malley, David – Partner of
    Frank Gehry   119
Open space acquisition
    program, Portland OR   139

Pennsylvania, University of   7
Petroleum-free new town,
    Dubai   140
Population, US, Projections for
    2030   57
_____ Growth 200 million in 1967
    to 300 million in 2007   183
Portland, OR   30
_____ What's so special?   138
Poverty, The War on   58
Public housing   101

Rapkin, Chet, Prof. University of
    Pennsylvania,
    Columbia Work Group   117
Regional Planning Councils   29

Revenue bonds, source of National Partnership for MetroCities' funds   99

Richmond, CA   5

Rockefeller, David, Chase Bank, Columbia financing   111

Rockefeller, Nelson, New York Governor, supporter of New South Richmond project   167

Roosevelt, Eleanor   17

Roosevelt, Franklin, President   25
    New Deal   39

Rouse, James, Founder of The Rouse Company and Columbia MD   17, 111
____ Personal Philosophy   44
    Berkeley speech   115

Rusk, David, Mayor of Albuquerque, researcher of metropolitan areas, Author *Inside Game, Outside Game*   41
    Baltimore Unbound   135

Sandtown-Winchester, Baltimore neighborhood   45

Sears, Paul, PhD Yale Ecologist, first consultant to Columbia MD   116

Section 8 housing vouchers   58

Simon Company   70

SmartGrowth   60

South Richmond, Plan for southern portion of Staten Island   10

Sprawl Kills by Joel Hirschorn   31

St. Louis, The Greater St. Louis Blues   50

Sunbelt, Too Hot   131

Sunfest   8

Sustainable communities 66

Tennenbaum, Robert, Columbia MD architect-planner   7, 15, 111

Thompson, Wayne   15
    Columbia Work Group   117

Tilton, L. Deming   15

Timetable for MetroCities   141

University of California at Berkeley, Department of City and Regional Planning   7

Urban Stress   33

Urbanitis – A definition   3

U.S. Census Bureau   53

Village of Cross Keys, Baltimore   5

Voorhees, Alan, DC Transportation expert, Columbia Work Group   116

Water, Water, the Floridan Aquifer   144

Watson, Raymond, President, The Irvine Ranch   109

Webber, Mel Professor UC Berkeley   108

West, Edward   15

Wheaton, William   15

Wind Power   88

Wilde, Frazier, Connecticut General
  Life Insurance Co.   110
Wise, Harold   15
Woodlands, TX 110
Wurster, Catherine Bauer   15

Yaro, Robert, New York Regional
  Plan Assoc.   128
Year 2000 Plan, National Capital
  Planning Commission   10,
  147

Made in the USA